"I had read other 'self-help' books but had not seen or heard of a book that encompassed every aspect of my emotional being as this one does.

Not only was I receiving amazing advice, I was getting to know Donna, the person. I feel deeply privileged to have benefited from her teachings. The chapter 'The Jigsaw Puzzle' resonated with me to such an extent that after I finished reading it, I immediately took the action Donna had suggested and my life changed that day."

~ Jude Herman – London Ontario Canada ~

STRATEGIES for HAPPINESS

How to Achieve Your Happiness Potential

DONNA L. HEDLEY, BRE

First Edition Copyright © 2009 by Donna Hedley
All rights reserved. No part of this book may be used or reproduced in any manner whatsoever without written permission of the author.

Exception: a reviewer or researcher who may quote brief passage in a review or research document with full credit given to the author.

Care has been taken to trace ownership of copyright material contained in this book. The author will gladly receive any information that will enable her to rectify any reference or credit line in subsequent editions. Although both the author and publisher have made every effort to ensure the accuracy and completeness of information contained in this book, we assume no responsibility for errors, inaccuracies, omissions, or any inconsistency herein. Any slights of people, places, or organizations are unintentional. For more information, visit: www.strategies4happiness.com or www.donnahedley.com

Library and Archives Canada Cataloguing in Publication

Hedley, Donna L., 1956-
    Strategies for happiness : how to achieve your happiness potential / Donna L. Hedley.

Includes bibliographical references.
ISBN 978-0-9811504-0-6

1. Happiness. 2. Self-actualization (Psychology). I. Title.

BF575.H27H44 2009   152.4'2   C2009-903898-6

Published by Sassy Sunflower Books, Ottawa ON, Canada

Sassy Sunflower Books.com

ATTENTION CORPORATIONS, UNIVERSITIES, COLLEGES, AND PROFESSIONAL ORGANIZATIONS: Quantity discounts are available on bulk purchases of this book for educational, gift purposes, or as premiums for increasing magazine subscriptions or renewals. Special books or book excerpts can also be created to fit specific needs. For information, please contact Sassy Sunflower Books at www.SassySunflowerBooks.com.

To Rebecca, Heather,
Kathleen, and Lynn

Thanks for
all the love,
learning, and laughter

Disclaimer

I want you to find happiness for yourself. For this reason, I present these strategies for your benefit and consideration, in the hope that they will empower you to think, grow and develop into the best you can be.

However, you need to take responsibility for your life, the decisions you make, and the actions you take. I can't guarantee these ideas will work for you. Nor can I predict how they will affect your life. I can only present them for you to consider.

These are just my views and opinions. It is not my intention to provide specific medical or psychiatric advice as I am not a doctor or mental health provider..

I don't necessarily endorse any specific organization, company, or product – just your right to choose happiness.

The sole purpose is to share options so that you can decide what is best for you. It is not my intention to have you take any action without consideration of a competent professional. Understand then that I disclaim any responsibility for any liability, loss, or risk, personal or otherwise, which is incurred as a consequence, directly or indirectly, of the use and application of any of the contents of this book.

Contents

Acknowledgements ix

My Story 1

Happiness 14

Gratitude 28

Personal Power 35

Give Yourself Permission 46

Enough is Enough 52

Don't Take It Personally 63

Relinquish Rightness 68

Forgive 74

Pursue Your Passion 90

Overcome the Judge 103

Radical Humility 109

Be Independent 114

Choose Courage 121

Take Control	127
Create Your Own Meaning	131
Be Self-Centred	137
The Power of Choice	146
Body Balance	160
Embrace Failure	168
Learn the Lesson of Pain	174
Purge the Pity Party	178
The Jigsaw Puzzle	183
Eradicate Envy	193
Create Your Opportunities	199
Focus on What You Want	203
Your Story	208
Desiderata	210
Must Read Books	213
About the Author	217
Websites	218

ACKNOWLEDGEMENTS

Thank you to all the wonderful people who have helped to make this book a reality.

Thanks, Ben, Janice and Jude, for helping the words make more sense through the editing process.

Thanks to Janice, Debbie, Vicky, TJ, Mary, Margareth, Ruth, Sarah, The Aunts: Lilie and Kay, Lalita, Susan, and Carol for being sweet and supportive, true and loyal friends. You are all among those rare and wonderful people that can make one feel truly special just being in your presence. Thanks for all the delicious encouragement, love, support, and constructive comments that have made this project all the better for knowing you.

Thanks to my Mom and Dad, who are truly marvelous people. I am honoured and grateful to be your daughter.

And thank you Ken, for being the sweetest of men and putting up with my craziness for all these years.

My Story

My Grandmother once said to me, "Be good. But if you can't be good, be good at it." I love to see the surprise and shock on people's faces, thinking about my Grandma, such a sweet and gentle, good church woman, saying such a thing. I'm not sure that she fully understood how those words could be taken. Or maybe she did. . .

Here is how I like to interpret it. Live your life to the fullest. Don't settle for second best. Make the most with what you have while endeavoring to be the best that you can be. When things don't go just as you planned, make the most of the experience. Take the nasty that can happen and learn from it.

> Happiness is a choice, not a chance!
> **Donna Hedley**

This is what I hope for you. I want you to make the most of your life – to realize that you can decide to live the fullest, richest, and best life possible. To live life on your terms. It's not about just finding the good in the bad or making the best out of a raw deal but of taking the bull by the horns and declaring what you expect your life to be and claiming it for your own.

Strategies for Happiness

Let me share with you a bit about myself. My story begins in a tiny borough of Toronto, named East York. I was born to Evelyn and John Hedley. My sisters, Lynn and Kathleen were ready and waiting to be both my joy and torment, as siblings often are. I remember many happy days playing on the street with my childhood sweetheart Chuckie (or at least I wanted him to be), and other assorted chums: Peter and the two Davids. Having lots of fun playing hide and seek, setting off fire crackers, picnics at Taylor Creek, I was, for the most part, optimistic and care-free.

Despite all the happy times, I somehow didn't feel like I belonged. From a very young age, I felt on the fringe. I don't remember exactly when this feeling took hold, however, the older I became, the more isolated I felt.

The Hedley family – Dad, Mom, Lynn, Kathleen and baby makes five

My Story

I blamed my parents. Somehow, it was their fault I didn't belong to the world. I felt like I was unwanted by my family – that they just tolerated me because I existed – if they had their choice, they would rather have someone else. (Before I go any further, I must explain that I have since come to the conclusion that I am one of the luckiest kids on the planet to have the parents and family that I have. Just wanted to clear that up.)

> The basic thing is that everyone wants happiness, no one wants suffering. And happiness mainly comes from our own attitude, rather than from external factors. If your own mental attitude is correct, even if you remain in a hostile atmosphere, you feel happy.
>
> **The Dalai Lama**

By the time I hit Grade 3, because of poor concentration, my grades began to suffer. As a result, my parents were persuaded to put me into a special class for slow learners – a move I think my mother always regretted. I don't remember much about that class except that the group was small (nine prisoners, eh, I mean students), from Grades 1 to 3.

I was the Grade 3 kid. I remember doing a lot of painting and playing – not much learning. We had a separate recess from the regular kids. We would have a naptime under our desks after lunch. I was picked up and taken home in a taxi, which started my weight problems.

My mother was not happy with the situation. She complained to the school about my progress and what I was learning (and not learning) and how I was actually regressing. As a result, the school

STRATEGIES FOR HAPPINESS

placed me into a regular Grade 3 class for the afternoon. That is where I learned to write longhand (yes sir, no more printing for me). I will always be grateful to my mother for standing up for me the way she did and fighting to ensure I got a proper education. It was just one example of her loving care.

The next year I was back in the regular school system, however much damage had been done. My school life went downhill. My grades were never good, and my social life was in shambles. No one would play with me; I still don't know why. It could be that I was haunted by the stigma of having been in a "special" Grade 3 class.

> Friendship is the golden thread that ties the heart of all the world.
> **John Evelyn**

In addition, I had started to put on weight – not a lot, but enough to be noticed and teased about and I had an enormous overbite. The only people willing to play with me were the Grade 1 and 2 kids. That fact only enhanced the idea that I was not to associate with.

I did have some friends. There was Janice, my friend from Sunday School. We met when we were about twelve. We were aware of each other from church, but it wasn't until I started going to Sunday School that we really got to know each other.

From the beginning, she was so very loving and kind to me, but I always felt that she said she liked me only because it was her Christian duty to do so. I was so hungry for love that I didn't care. I would take what I could get. I know now that that was not so – that she really did (does) care for me – but that's another story.

My Story

Such a cutie

At the time, it was hard for me to believe that anyone could love me. It's my belief that Janice saved my life. In spite of my doubts, it seemed to me that she was the one person who seemed to think I was okay. This gave me hope to keep going and to not give up. I often wonder what path I would have taken if she had not been in my life. This, of course, was just my perception of how things were, not reality. I had many people who loved me, but at the time, I couldn't see it.

Through Sunday School, I also made another life-long friend, Debbie. She is the kind of solid, no nonsense, kind and gentle person you need to help you through the mess of life. Thanks to both of you.

Back on the school front, a new student joined our class. Her name was Margaret and she was from Scotland. She didn't know me or my reputation. When she came into the class and was introduced, I got a brilliant idea. I said to myself, "Why not get to her before everyone else does, and make her my friend?!"

STRATEGIES FOR HAPPINESS

My first car

My plan worked. I went out of my way to be friendly to her. She seemed to really like me. It helped that she lived just a few houses down from me. We did a lot of things together outside of school, as well as hanging out at school. For some reason, she didn't seem to let the other kids affect her view of me. Even our parents got along really well. Their friendship outlasted ours. When her family decided to move, I was heart-broken.

In Junior High, I continued to be an outcast. I was taunted about my weight, teeth, appearance, and so on. The problem was, I believed they were right and on some level, I agreed with them.

In Grade 7, there was a boy who sat behind me who would constantly kick me. I rarely complained. I had found out that complaining often got me in more trouble than the problem that

My Story

I was complaining about. It seemed that whenever I stood up for myself, I ended up worse off. I call this the Timothy Factor.

The concept of the Timothy Factor was born when I was walking to school one day and was joined by Timothy V., your basic run-of-the-mill bully. Timothy started to kick me and though I told him to stop, he just kept kicking. Finally, in desperation, I kicked him back, which only made him continue his attack.

I decided I was going to do something about this once and for all. When I got to school, I complained to the teachers. They took Timothy aside and talked to him. They took me aside and asked me if I had kicked him. In my anger and pain, all I could think about was that he had started kicking me, with no provocation. So I said no. I had forgotten that I had kicked him back.

Beach bums

STRATEGIES FOR HAPPINESS

As it happens, there was a girl up the street from us who had come out of her house just as I, in frustration, had kicked back. She testified that I had started the quarrel. So, the result was that I was the one who got into trouble. I was reprimanded for starting a fight with Timothy. My name was put into the book (the dreaded book – if your name appeared three times, you were punished with the strap).

The entire event was humiliating and painful. I returned to my class in tears. What made it even more humiliating was my class laughed at me because they assumed that I was crying as a result of having been punished. What I learned from this experience was if you stand up for yourself, in the end, you are blamed anyway, so why bother. This way of thinking was totally false, but a belief nonetheless.

> No matter how dull, or how mean, or how wise a man is, he feels that happiness is his indisputable right.
>
> ***Helen Keller***

I now understand that my problems were created because of a very faulty belief system. It was not that my family and friends didn't love me but that I *believed* they didn't and therefore I got what I deserved. Because I didn't think I was likable, I taught others that they didn't have to like me. They would do and say hateful things, and I accepted it. I agreed. This further fed their view of me. It's one of those "vicious circle" things.

For example, one day when I was walking up the street, Susan V. (sister to the dreaded Timothy V.) stepped out in front of me. She and a friend had pushed a wagon onto the sidewalk and began to taunt

My Story

Dad, Mom and me

me. They indicated that I was not allowed to pass by. I cried as they continued to tease and taunt.

I know what you're thinking. Why didn't I just step onto the road and walk around the wagon? Or turn around and go the other way and ignore them? My response is, I don't know. It seemed such an insurmountable problem to me then. I was so upset and accepted what they were saying was true. I agreed with them and on a subconscious level choose to believe it was true.

In Grade 7, I had my first boyfriend, George W. We sat together on the bus when our class went to Black Creek Pioneer Village. It was here that I first understood the power of the feminine. I admired a plastic whistle in the shape of a log, with a bird perched on it. I fingered it lovingly. It worked because he bought it for me. He

STRATEGIES FOR HAPPINESS

Me with Chuckie

Hanging with my Dad

The budding movie star

Nature lover

10

My Story

wanted to take me on a date to a movie, but my parents wouldn't allow it. I was too young. Instead, we went for a long walk down the valley in Taylor Creek Park. We had a nice time lying on the grass, looking at the stars.

Soon after that, when I spoke to him at school, he turned a cold shoulder to me. Then, he joined the others in taunting me. I never knew what happened, but I suspect that the other kids filled him in on my reputation, and peer pressure was more important than I was.

After high school I worked, went to college, married, had children, divorced, and grew up. Through it all, I had many great times, wonderful friends, and many highs and lows. However, I continued to feel on the fringe. In 1992, I experienced a major depression. I was having problems with my job. My sister Kathleen was terminally ill. I was having anxiety attacks constantly – what I like to call my D'oh moments (I identified a lot with Homer Simpson).

> Sometimes life can be as bitter as dragon tears. But whether dragon tears are bitter or sweet depends entirely on how each man perceives them.
>
> ***Chinese proverb***

You know the saying about someone being so down that a dark cloud follows them everywhere they go? Well, that was me. I just knew that cloud was following me and almost believed that if I just turned around fast enough, I would actually see it.

It all changed when I decided I had had enough and had to take action to change. It was at that time when I decided to write a book, which led to research and finding new ways of thinking. It has been

STRATEGIES FOR HAPPINESS

Playtime with my Grandma

an exciting journey. I realize I am not the only one who has gone through this, but this is my story.

My life was not all doom and gloom. I was blessed with a loving family and some very special friends and have had many wonderful experiences and joys.

I wanted to share the dark times because we all have them. I know now that the people in my life did what they did because they didn't know any better. I came to realize that to a big extent, I taught them how to treat me. But who taught me? Why did I come to believe what I did about myself? Why did I learn to agree with all the negative stuff people thought of me?

What has happened in the past is irrelevant. What is important is where I am right now. What has happened has happened, and I

My Story

can't change that. What I can change is how I look at my life in the here and now and in what direction I want to take my life for the future.

I have learned that my happiness is up to me – it's my responsibility. I can choose to develop happiness, or I can choose to stay in misery. My hope is that you can identify with my pain and through that also identify with my joy and learn that happiness is truly a choice – one I hope you will make.

Happiness

What is happiness? That is for you to decide. For me, happiness is a state of mind. It's a mindset free from fear, self-pity, and negative thinking. It's a way of thinking that says, yes, the world is unfair, and often horrible things happen, but I can rise above it all and still enjoy life. In a nutshell, happiness is freedom.

In the book, "The Art of Happiness: A Handbook For Living" Tenzin Gyatso, the 14th Dalai Lama says, ". . .the highest happiness is when one reaches the stage of Liberation, at which there is no more suffering. That's genuine, lasting happiness. True happiness relates more to the mind and heart."

He continues by saying,

> *I believe that the very purpose of our life is to seek happiness. That is clear. Whether one believes in religion or not, whether one believes in this religion or that religion, we are all seeking something better in life. So, I think, the very motion of our life is toward happiness. . .*

HAPPINESS

Happiness is *energy*. When you are in a state of happiness, you are energized. You are motivated to create, move, and develop. Happiness is *purpose*. Those who are truly happy know their lives count for something. They are creating their world – achieving their destiny. Whether their purpose is to write a book and share their joy with others, find a cure for cancer, teach, or train and mold their children to be the best they can be, happiness abounds.

> You can either be happy or sad, and I'm always a lot happier when I'm happy!
>
> **Anonymous**

Happiness is a *choice*. We may not be able to control all the things that happen to us or come into our lives, but we can choose to decide how we will respond to them. The events and people that affect our life are just facts. The emotion we attached to these facts are up to us to decide. We give them meaning.

Our choices have consequences – joy or misery – freedom or bondage. The more I research and develop as a person and expand my happiness potential, the more I am free from being chained to bitterness, hurt, and self-pity. Freedom is such an exquisite feeling. I am still on my journey – I don't think it ever ends but it's a journey filled with wonder, hope, and joy.

I can't tell you what is going to develop your *Happiness Potential*. That is your journey. What I will tell you is that you have the power, the ability, and the responsibility to find it. I am going to give you ideas that can help you to find it in your life, but it's up to you to make the effort to see what works for you.

Strategies for Happiness

Everyone is born with a certain kind of character. Then, as he/she goes through life, events happen that can modify that character, either for the good or bad. Your life is shaped by heredity, environment and even more powerful, the choices you make.

Our bodies are made up of many chemicals which need to be in balance in order for us to function properly. Heredity, environment, and choices can affect this balance. How we choose to care for our body or manipulate our environment can also affect the balance and dramatically influence our overall view of the world.

Of all the things that shape our lives, choices have the greatest effect. We often do not realize we have made choices or that we even have options. We don't try to improve because we are under the false belief that things are the way they are, and we can't do anything about them. This inaction is a choice as well, and may be the worst choice of all.

We all have what I like to call *Happiness Potential*. Some people seem to have a more natural tendency to be happy than others, but we all have the potential for happiness. Sometimes it seems that some of us need to work at it harder than others. This is because on some level, we have agreed to believe lies about ourselves.

The purpose of this book is to share ideas, concepts, and practical strategies that can help you choose a better life, to find the truth about our magnificence. Much of what I share here can be backed by research. However, this is not my focus. It's not as important to know why it works – just that it does if you let it.

These ideas may not be new. You may have heard them a million times before. Often it takes a number of times in the

HAPPINESS

telling before you actually internalize ideas and make them your own. That's when the miracles start.

Why Should You Care About Happiness?

When you develop your Happiness Potential, you are excited and pumped each day, you have a sense of purpose and you enjoy what you do – you have learned how to deal with the nasty that life can throw at you. This is what it means to *succeed*.

> Success in life is becoming what you want to be.
> **Wallace D. Wattles**

Does this sound selfish? Actually, it's the most unselfish thing you can do. If fact, I think everyone should be self-centred, in a constructive way. If we concentrate on what makes us the most happy and healthy, our joy will overflow and touch others. You can then share this joy with others, who in turn can also share and spread the joy even more.

When people talk about happiness, they often refer to the people, the places, and the things that make them feel good. Or they think about pleasure. Though these things can be good, they are not the point of happiness. The kind of happiness I am talking about is not just a good feeling, but an overall mindset – a way of being.

Happiness is made up of three basic components: Awareness, Attitude, and Action.

STRATEGIES FOR HAPPINESS

Awareness: What do you think about yourself?

The first step is awareness. If you are not aware of the thoughts you are thinking, and of the options that are available to you, you cannot begin to figure out what action you need to take in order to change. If you don't know what the problem is, it is difficult to solve it.

> Happiness is the only good. The time to be happy is now. The place to be happy is here. The way to be happy is to make others so.
>
> **_Robert Green Ingersoll_**

Awareness is understanding the way you are thinking and viewing yourself as well as seeing how it affects the quality of your life. Do your thoughts enrich you, or are they destructive?

A dictionary definition of awareness is "having or showing realization, perception, or knowledge; Awareness implies vigilance in observing or alertness in drawing inferences from what one experiences." We need to be *vigilant* and learn to tune into our innermost being. We need to be able to gauge our mental state, and become crystal clear about the things that are causing us pain, and then decide what to do about them.

I've talked to people who say, "This is the way I am. I can't change." They have already decided that they can't change, so they don't. They are not yet aware that they have options. Once a person is open to the reality that options exist, they start moving towards what is possible, even if it doesn't happen right away.

Happiness

Our thoughts reveal what our attitude is about ourselves and our world. Being conscious of our thoughts help us determine what beliefs we need to modify in order to realize our happiness potential.

Attitude: What do you believe about yourself?

Happiness is a mindset – a way of thinking. What is your present state of mind, your attitude about you and your life?

Once you are aware of your thoughts, you need to examine what your attitudes are. No great change can happen unless you are aware of your thoughts and have claimed that you are responsible for what you have chosen to believe.

Others may negatively affect your life, but only you can decide what the outcome will be. Taking responsibility does not mean you are taking blame, it just means that you are taking control of the outcome.

What are the attitudes we hold about ourselves and those around us? What do we need to change, embrace, enhance and celebrate? Having claimed responsibility, you need to look at all the attitudes you own.

Happiness comes from having a positive, constructive mindset. Filling your being with love, gratitude, appreciation, and courage will build a defence against the nasty of the world. Nasty will still get in, but with the proper attitude, you are better suited to defend yourself.

I find that many people say they can't change, when in reality, on some deep level, they just don't want to change. They have

Strategies for Happiness

justified in their minds that their behaviour and attitudes are normal and unchangeable because they are either enjoying the negative pattern or because it just seems like too much work to change.

It's like being stuck in the mud. It is hard to pull yourself out, but once you do, you are free. You can have a shower, wash off the dirt, and it feels good. So many people would rather be stuck in the mud of the negative than put in the effort to pull themselves out. I don't know about you, but a shower sure sounds good to me.

Our beliefs dictate what actions we allow ourselves to take. If we believe we can accomplish something, we will do it. Otherwise, we just won't try. As Henry Ford once said, "If you think you can do a thing or think you can't do a thing, you're right."

The wonderful thing is, that we have choice, and we can choose to change our attitudes about anything, as long as we make that choice and then take action to make it happen.

Action: What do you choose to do about your thoughts and beliefs?

The most important thing we need to become aware of is that we *do* have the ability to choose – we can choose to change our belief system. We can choose to change the way we react to negative situations.

We can choose to accept that there are some things in our lives that are beyond our control but at the same time understand that we always have options. Or we can choose to give up and drown in our pain.

Happiness

Every one of us has issues, and it is important that we deal with them. Sometimes our greatest block to resolving issues is our own belief system. If we believe we cannot solve our own problems, there is no power on earth that will change how we see the problem. Only you can decide to make the changes you need in order to break through. You do have a choice. Choose to be happy, and then find the tools to make it happen. It is in your hands. Building happiness – reaching toward your personal Happiness Potential – should be one of your primary goals.

> We all find ourselves in situations that at times seem hopeless. And, we all have the choice to do nothing or take action.
>
> **Catherine Pulsifer**

Some of you may remember the old commercial saying "Don't wait till spring, do it now!" That is what proactivity is all about. Dr. Dan Baker, author of the book *What Happy People Know,* says "Happy people participate in their own destinies and forge their own happiness. They don't wait for events or other people to make them happy. They're not passive victims."

Once you are aware of what your attitudes are, take action! There are three types of action you can take. First, you can *develop positive characteristics,* such as love, gratitude, and generosity. Second, you can *minimize your misery* by no longer doing the things that cause you pain, such as holding a grudge, feeling sorry for yourself, or complaining. And last, you can take the kinds of action that will *enhance good health*, both physically and mentally, such as eating right, exercising and meditation.

STRATEGIES FOR HAPPINESS

The World Needs More Happy People

My happiness is very important to me. That is why I decided to make the pursuit of happiness one of my highest priorities. My goal is not only to make sure I have the best possible life, but also that I take what I have learned and share it with others. The more truly happy people there are, the better the world becomes.

When I was depressed, I started to examine myself to become aware of what was happening and figure out a solution. I have a number of theories as to why it happened. I believe it was partly due to a chemical imbalance in my body. Also, I became aware of the many negative and self-absorbing attitudes I had learned and accepted. I also had some very negative outside situations that were beyond my control. I took action. I made it my purpose and passion to research and find practical ways to improve my level of happiness and to share it with everyone.

Even if you consider that your life is pretty good, there is always room for improvement. The universe is a large place, and from what we hear, it's getting even bigger by the second. Happiness is like the universe. There is always room to grow and improve. It seems to me to be limitless.

The happier we are, the more we spread happiness to others, who in turn spread it even more. It is like a giant "Happiness Network". If our happiness was a primary goal in our life, and we in turn shared it with those around us, the world would be a better place.

I like things to be simple, with step-by-step instructions. I like learning by going through steps and following a logical series of ideas or events. Knowing this, I started to collect and develop strategies

HAPPINESS

that have helped me in my journey – practical concepts and ideas that if incorporated, can transform your life. There is nothing scientific about these strategies, although, as I mentioned before, there is a lot of scientific evidence to support them. They come from insight, experience, and practice.

Often life, well, sucks. There is no guarantee that we will have a full, rich, and happy life. There are often hardships and trials. However, if we can acquire tools that can make us aware of our state of mind and our options as well as empower our attitude, and then take the appropriate actions to propel ourselves towards becoming the best we can be, we will be well on our way to being a happier, healthier individuals. The Strategies for Happiness described in this book are among such tools.

> Happiness is man's greatest aim in life. Tranquility and rationality are the cornerstones of happiness.
>
> **Epicurus**

The purpose of this book is not to fix you. I can't do that, nor would I even dare to try. The purpose is to help you realize that you have the right, the responsibility, and the tools to fix your life for yourself. I want you to become aware of your own situation, for good or bad so that you may make choices that can change your life.

My goal is to provide you with many different ideas allowing you to take action, thus increase your happiness potential. Some may work better than others, but I am sure there is something in this bag of tricks that will change your life. I want to make you think, to take responsibility and control for your life, to say, "Hey, here's

STRATEGIES FOR HAPPINESS

something that may be useful to me," and then to go and try it. I want you to live life on your own terms.

We are all individuals and need to find our own way. Each of the over six billion people on the face of this earth have their own idea of what happiness is. That means you need to find out what works for you, and not be manipulated by other people and their ideas.

> Happiness is the meaning and the purpose of life, the whole aim and end of human existence.
>
> **Aristotle**

It is important for you to be aware of your feelings. Don't be afraid of them or ignore them, nor should you allow them to control you. When dealing with negative feelings, you need to be fully aware of the problem in order to handle it properly. If you don't face it fully, it's difficult to make the necessary decisions and take the actions giving you the power to overcome.

Action is always better than inaction. With action, you will at least be moving toward something. Don't worry about making a mistake. The beauty about taking action is that you always have the option to evaluate the results and redirect when needed.

Mistakes often end up being blessings in disguise. Another great line by Henry Ford is, "Even a mistake may turn out to be the one thing necessary to a worthwhile achievement." When you are driving down the road, you are constantly correcting yourself. If you didn't, you would soon drive into the ditch. Take action, correct your direction, adjusting your course as necessary and arrive somewhere. Otherwise, you will get nowhere very fast.

Happiness

There have been times where I just didn't feel like doing anything; I just didn't want to move. It was easier to wallow in my pain than to get moving. I was scared to do something because I didn't think I could do it well enough to achieve anything of value.

For example, I wanted to become a professional speaker in the Personal Development field. It's not just that I wanted to become a speaker, but I sincerely wanted to do something that was going to be of value to others and make their lives better. I wanted to do that through workshops, presentations, writing, and any other way I could find that would promote this purpose. In the past, I was concerned that I didn't have anything to offer. I believed that I didn't have the training or experience that many would consider necessary.

Then I realized that the way I should look at it was to do it just for fun – just for the joy of doing it. I decided to do it for the pleasure of it and not to worry about whether I was going to be a success in the eyes of the world. I would do things that I enjoyed and that I felt were going to be beneficial to me and those around me. This change in my thinking has given me such freedom.

Now I am doing whatever it takes to that end. I am not going to let fear keep me from my goal. No matter what happens on this journey, I have had a lot of fun and met a lot of great people. Most importantly, I've learned a lot about myself.

All the research I have been doing has transformed my life. With all that I am learning and teaching, I am filled with much gratitude and joy. I'm learning not to worry when I fall on my face, and when things happen that tick me off. Sometimes I forget and let myself get uptight about some of the negative things in my life. The reality is, nasty does happen, no matter how much you work at

STRATEGIES FOR HAPPINESS

it, and no matter how much you try to develop yourself as a person. As a happiness specialist, I still fall on my face once in a while and fail in the areas in which I am trying to succeed.

Some people say that failure is simply not succeeding, or that you only truly fail when you give up trying. I don't agree with this definition. There are times when you will not succeed in attaining what you set out to do. You find out it does not meet your expectations or do much to enhance your life. At that point, it is wise to let it go. This is not failure. This is learning and experiencing.

> Happiness is not in our circumstance but in ourselves. It is not something we see, like a rainbow, or feel, like the heat of a fire. Happiness is something we are.
>
> **John B. Sheerin**

The Secret to Happiness is... Love Yourself

The number one secret to happiness is to love yourself, fully, without reservation. If there's only one thing this book does for you, I hope it's that you come to a clear and full realization of the following fact: your level of happiness is in direct proportion to how happy you are with yourself. Consider the ideas I share and make it happen.

If you are not happy with yourself, you will never be happy with anything or anyone else in your life. If you are experiencing any measure of un-happiness, it's probably because you have not totally embraced the wonder of who you are.

Jesus said to love your neighbour as yourself. If you cannot love yourself, you will not be able to truly love your neighbour in any

HAPPINESS

meaningful way. Do whatever it takes to love yourself, to get over the pain and anger you store in your body. Work through the anger, the wrongs, the guilt, and the misconceptions. Forgive yourself. If you learn to love yourself in a real, authentic, and healthy way, you cannot fail in finding true happiness.

Not only will it ensure you a rich, full and satisfying life, but you will be in the best position possible for reaching out and helping others share your joy. If you live in a place of inner peace and harmony, you are in the best situation to make the best decisions and choices to achieve the best possible life.

Does this mean you will never feel pain, nor be upset or angry again? Probably not. However, the more you fall in love with yourself in a healthy and affirming way, the better equipped you will be to weather the storms that are sure to come your way.

I don't have all the answers; I never will. It doesn't matter if you or I know everything, as long as we become aware of the possibilities and make an effort to achieve them. Take that challenge, pursue your authentic happiness, make it a driving force in your life, and spread it out to all around you, thereby making the world a better place. I hope you find the freedom.

My life has been an education in learning to appreciate me. I have come a long way, and I don't know if I will ever 100% accept and love myself the way I would like to. Just because I am not perfect doesn't mean I should give up working to be the best I can be. I am still way ahead of where I was and excited about the possibilities of the future. I'm going places. You're welcome to join me.

GRATITUDE

There I was, stuck in the mud. It was 10 P.M., my class was finished, and everyone was gone. I had made the mistake of parking my car in the dirt lot beside the school, and it had rained. I got into the car, turned the ignition, and started to pull out. Except the car wouldn't move. Like the kiddie song, "The wheels on the bus go round and round, round and round, round and round", and this bus wasn't going anywhere.

What was I to do? There was no one there to help me, no classmates – nobody in the building could do anything. My friends did not live close enough to help. I was strapped for cash, and the thought of calling a company to tow my car away was very painful. To my wallet, I mean. Finally, I bit the bullet and made a call. I was told it would cost $50. Ouch!

After a short wait, a tow truck came rambling down the road. A friendly-faced man, reminiscent of Grizzly Adams, lumbered out of the truck. "Grizzly" quickly assessed the situation and pulled my car out in no time. I went to pay him and he waived it away. He just pulled me out a few feet – not really a tow – and he wouldn't take the money. He wouldn't even take a tip. I could have kissed him.

GRATITUDE

How did he know I was a single mother, struggling to make ends meet, and this simple act of kindness would help to feed my kids next week? I will always be grateful to Grizzly Adams and how he helped me that night.

Think of a time when someone has done something or said some kind words that just filled you with gratitude. You can't help but feel joy when your being is overflowing with the appreciation of a person, place or thing. It can literally push out any thoughts of anger or pain. Gratitude conquers all.

> Man is fond of counting his troubles, but he does not count his joys. If he counted them up as he ought to, he would see that every lot has enough happiness provided for it.
>
> **Fyodor Dostoevsky**

Sometimes, it's being grateful for what is NOT in our life.

He was the perfect man. Tall, smart, wise, kind and with such a powerful beautiful voice. I wanted so much to be Mrs. ___. It, however, was not to be. He saw me only as a friend. He was interested in someone else and that someone else became Mrs. ___.

We went our separate ways and time passed. I married, had children, got divorced, and went through many changes. Years later, we met again. It was nice to see him and his wife, exchange our stories and pictures of our children, and generally catch up on our lives. I looked at him, remembered how much I had dreamed of being married to him, and realized that I was very grateful it had not happened.

STRATEGIES FOR HAPPINESS

Don't get me wrong, he's still a great guy. He is a loving husband and father, still had a beautiful voice, still interesting and smart. I was glad I was not his wife.

I would not be who I am today if I had. I love where I am, who I have become. I think being married to him might have held me back. I was so grateful that I did not get what I wanted.

> Let us rise up and be thankful, for if we didn't learn a lot today, at least we learned a little, and if we didn't learn a little, at least we didn't get sick, and if we got sick, at least we didn't die; so, let us all be thankful.
>
> **Buddha**

Whether you are grateful for the things you have, for the things you don't have, or lessons learned, gratitude can fill your life with such joy that there isn't any room for pain.

What is gratitude? It's awareness and appreciation of what is good in our lives. Sometimes it's really obvious what we are grateful for. Other times we have to dig deeper to see evidence of reasons to be grateful. There is an abundance of reasons and sources for gratitude always around us. In addition to that, we can create it. We always have the power to create. When you have a problem seeing something to be grateful for, create reasons to be filled with gratitude.

In the book *What Happy People Know*, Dr. Dan Baker says that "Appreciation is the highest, purest form of love . . . that can blossom even when it is not returned." He further explains that "Appreciation asks for nothing, and gives everything." Appreciation will conquer fear. Happiness isn't the lack of problems or sorrows

GRATITUDE

but about having the ability to deal with life head on. Love gives you a source of power and strength in order to do that. Gratitude fills you with love.

Dr. Baker continues, "No matter what happens in life, there's always something left to love, and the love that remains is always stronger than anything that goes against it."

Gratitude comes from appreciation which is a form of love, maybe the best kind of love there is. When you learn to appreciate everything in your life, you fill your life with love. Love has the ability to conquer fear and give you a great source of power and strength to overcome it. True happiness means to be free, especially from fear. Developing gratitude can help you to obtain that freedom.

Appreciation creates love. Gratitude creates appreciation. Gratitude for all the blessings in your life will give you a foundation to handle life's ups and downs.

Never "should" yourself to gratitude. If you feel you "should" be grateful, it's not going to be real. Instead, create reasons to be grateful. Not because you have to, but because it's going to make your life full, rich and free. You can create gratitude by learning to appreciate what is in your life, the good and the bad. When you can find a way to appreciate everything, finding a reason and meaning for whatever is happening, you begin your journey to gratitude.

Gratitude is not dependent on a belief system of a higher power. If you believe in a higher power, and declare your gratitude to that higher power, excellent. If you don't believe in a higher power, you can still be thankful. Declare your gratitude to the universe.

It's as simple as saying *thank you*.

STRATEGIES FOR HAPPINESS

Appreciation Log

To help you develop this in your life, you can start an Appreciation Log. Get a notebook and start to write all the things you are grateful for. Writing them down helps you to focus and become clear as to all the things in your life that are wonderful. If there are some situations or relationships that are not so great, start to think about reasons to be grateful in relation to these things or people.

How often you write in your journal is up to you. Some people like to write each day. Others can only find the time to write every so often. Make a habit of setting aside some regular time for this exercise. Start your writing by finishing the sentence "Today, I am grateful for. . ." or "I appreciate that. . ." Not only will this be an exercise that will help you to build appreciation for your life, but it will be a reminder for you when you are facing dark times.

> Look to your health; and if you have it, praise God, and value it next to a good conscience; for health is the second blessing that we mortals are capable of; a blessing that money cannot buy.
>
> **Izaak Walton**

On those days when things don't go so well, you can leaf through your record of gratitude and refocus on what really matters. As you are writing in your log, ask yourself "What am a truly grateful for today?", "Who will I make a point of thanking today?" and "What things are blocking me from feeling grateful?"

Gratitude

Another idea is to start an Appreciation Log for the special people in your life. You could create one that is just for your children, your spouse, or maybe a friend. Keep track of the ways that person brings you pleasure, what you love and appreciate about him/her. This is not only a good exercise for you, but when you share it with that loved one, it can be a source of joy for both of you – something that will always be treasured.

Thank You Notes

Consider writing thank you notes. Every Christmas, my Aunts always send us a thank you letter. It didn't matter that we just saw them and they had already thanked us verbally a number of times for the humble little gift we gave them. They still write us a nice letter and tell us how much they have enjoyed the gift.

You don't have to wait for a special occasion to write a thank you note. Make it a habit to send a note to someone you know on a weekly or monthly basis. Thank others for how they have touched your life or how you have seen them touch others. Or just thank them for being, period. Maybe you don't know the person that well, but the fact that you took the time to think of him/her will bring joy.

Though saying thank you verbally or even by e-mail is nice, it is such a nice touch to send an actual card in the mail. It takes a little more effort, but is something the recipient will really appreciate.

Random Acts of Kindness

When you interact with people, whether they are family or strangers, always treat them with respect and kindness. Acts

STRATEGIES FOR HAPPINESS

of kindness to those around you will generate appreciation and gratitude. It doesn't matter if you don't get anything out of it. What matters is that your act will bring joy to someone else. Even if the person does not act kindly in return, you know you did your part. What you will experience is a feeling of joy that you took the time to share with others.

> Gratefulness is the key to a happy life that we hold in our hands, because if we are not grateful, then no matter how much we have we will not be happy – because we will always want to have something else or something more.
>
> **Brother David Steindl-Rast**

Be careful that you don't put a price tag on your acts of kindness. Just because you do something nice, don't expect the recipient will be grateful back. Remember, you are doing something for the purpose of spreading joy, not so that someone will thank you.

If you do things that generate gratitude in you, the idea may extend to others, who in turn will develop gratitude. Pay it forward.

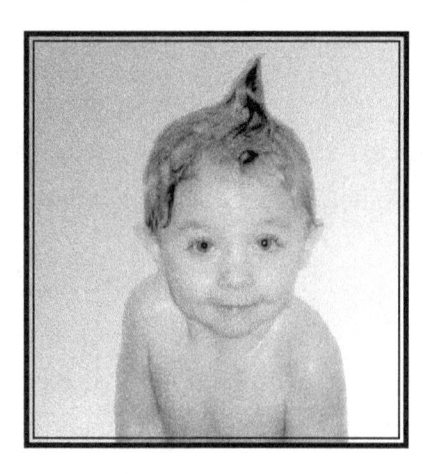

Personal Power

It was a great opportunity. I had been made manager of an entire department. Okay, so I was the only one in that department, it was still a great opportunity.

I threw myself into the job with great enthusiasm. I worked hard, did a great job, and felt a wonderful sense of satisfaction. My boss was pleased. My co-workers were pleased. Well, except for one person.

This individual made it very clear that she did not like me, did not support me, or see that I was of any value. She hated my guts. She was professional in all her interactions and dealings with me, but I could feel the anger and disgust boiling underneath, which of course made things uncomfortable at times.

Had I done anything to deserve this treatment? Was this fair? No, but in reality life is often not fair. It often seems to frustrate our personal sense of logic. What seemed so unfair and illogical to me made perfect sense to her.

This woman hated me, and that was a fact. The problem was I let it get to me. I tried my best to accept the fact that she did not like me and I did the best job I could in spite of it, but there would

STRATEGIES FOR HAPPINESS

be times when my sense of right or wrong made me go crazy trying to figure it out or trying to fix it. I let go of my personal power and allowed her to have control over me by accepting the idea that things were not as they should be.

"It's just not fair! It's not right the way they treat me! I don't deserve this! I have rights, you know!"

Does this sound familiar?

It's so easy to blame those around us for causing the pain in our lives. It's much easier than claiming responsibility for our lives and how we react to events. It's impossible to change others to suit our needs, so don't even try.

When someone causes us pain, we must make a decision to deal with it within ourselves. This doesn't mean we change our beliefs to conform to others, but that we need to adjust our attitude and reaction to best deal with any situation. Claiming your personal power and taking responsibility for your reactions to the situation will help you to deal with life's frustration.

Dan Baker, author of *What Happy People Know*, says that we should avoid what he calls the VERBs. They will destroy your life. The VERBs are:

V - Victimization

E - Entitlement

R - Rescue

B - Blame

PERSONAL POWER

Victimization

Think of a time when you have felt like you were a victim. When we allow ourselves to be victims in any situation, we are not in control because we give our power away to others. That is why it's so important to take responsibility for our thoughts and actions. Again, we can't control how other people act, but we can choose to respond in a constructive way instead of giving into the temptation of a knee-jerk reaction.

I understand the seductiveness of victimhood. There is a certain pleasure to being the victim, the hero or heroine of the drama of your life. The problem is, a victim is giving away their power to someone else and is therefore at their mercy. You need to ask yourself if you want to allow others to control and manipulate you, or, be the one in control of your life and well-being?

> When a milestone is conquered, the subtle erosion called entitlement begins its consuming grind. The team regards its greatness as a trait and a right. Half hearted effort becomes habit and saps a champion.
>
> ***Pat Riley***

There are times when things happen and we feel that it's not our fault. The temptation is to say, "Poor me!" and wallow in self-pity. It's a natural reaction to scream "It's not fair!" Whether it's fair or not, anger and self-pity will take its toll on you, even playing havoc on your health.

The Institute of HeartMath® (www.heartmath.org), founded by Doc Childre, is a nonprofit organization that helps people

STRATEGIES FOR HAPPINESS

find balance between their mind and heart in life's activities. In their book *The HeartMath Solution*, Childre and Howard Martin, Executive Vice President of HeartMath LLC, say that "Resentment, anger, frustration, worry, disappointment – negative emotional states, justified or not, take a toll on your heart, brain and body. Don't let justified emotions rob your health and well-being."

Entitlement

Our society has taught us to feel entitled to the things we have or to the things we think we should have. Credit cards have been a big factor in creating a "society of entitlement". Because people have the ability to purchase things they want immediately, they get instant gratification and a sense of importance. The problem is they still have to pay for the items they purchase. After awhile, they get to thinking that this gives them the right to have items, whether they need them or not. When they can't have them right away, they scream, "Foul play!" Entitlement breeds discontent.

> Don't go around saying the world owes you a living. The world owes you nothing. It was here first.
>
> **Mark Twain**

We are taught to fight for our *rights*. I believe that we don't have any rights. In fact, we are entitled to nothing, but we do have the opportunity to acquire everything whether it be material or spiritual. Entitlement is the sense that I should have things just because I want them. On the other hand, opportunity is the sense of power that I have to take action and achieve my goals.

Personal Power

For instance, we are not entitled to own a house. However, we do possess the ability and the opportunity to do whatever it takes to acquire one. We can find a job, earn and save up enough money, make the down payment, etc. Some individuals who receive social assistance get into a habit of expecting to be taken care of. They may get free money, but this does not free their spirit. Entitlement is a weight that holds you down.

Rescue

Have you ever been in a bad situation, and instead of taking action to overcome it, sat in self-pity hoping that someone would come along and take care of it for you? I know I have. Sometimes we need help, and there is nothing wrong with accepting it when it does come your way, but it's a cop-out to just give up and expect others to take care of you. You might be waiting a very long time. The American economist and social commentator Thomas Sowell said:

> *We should listen first and foremost to our own experience . . . We should stop looking for saviors . . . Society has not existed for thousands of years because it had a succession of saviors. It's existed because it has institutions and processes through which people can realize their own goals.*

Blame

It's so easy to blame those around us for causing the pain in our lives. It's much easier than looking within ourselves and seeing

Strategies for Happiness

how we can change things. We can't change others to suit our needs, so we have to look within ourselves to see how we can change. This does not mean that we should just give in and let people get away with things. In fact, I suggest that everyone needs to be held accountable. However, it's important to understand that since we can't change others, if someone causes us pain, we must make a decision on how to deal with it.

> He who angers you conquers you.
>
> **Elizabeth Kenny**

I once knew a couple who met at college and got married. It had been his dream to graduate and become an assistant pastor of a small country church near where he grew up. His wife told me their story.

"The senior pastor of the church was a very charming and energetic man who had started and ran three churches. My husband, being new to the ministry, was young, enthusiastic, and excited to serve God. He had looked forward to the day that he would be able to do the work of the church. Instead, he was relegated to doing menial tasks, such as printing the bulletins and changing the sign on the church lawn. He would start the service on Sunday morning, and when the senior pastor came, the older man would take over."

The young pastor was somewhat disappointed that after his education, and in spite of his enthusiasm, he was given so little work to do and so little encouragement and direction. It wasn't that the work assigned to him was below him. He was willing and wanting to serve however he could. However, he had more in him

Personal Power

that was being wasted. It was frustrating that after all his training, his skills and talents were being ignored.

The painful part was that, for some reason, the senior pastor seemed to see the younger man as a threat, and did his utmost to chastise and belittle instead of nurture and mentor. He seemed to think that my friend was trying to take over, which was far from the truth.

My friend continued her story. "My husband was hurt by these actions. He was humble enough to realize that in such a situation, you needed to start slow, learn, and grow, but it wasn't like that. The senior pastor seemed to have come to dislike my husband and did whatever he could to make sure he didn't succeed."

"I remember being so angry about the way my husband was being treated. I had a hard time being in the same place at the same time with this man whom I viewed as being very un-Christlike in his manner. Then one day I realized what was happening to me. I blamed him for our problems and my anger. I allowed his actions and attitudes to take control of me through my anger. When I realized this, I chose to stop my negative way of thinking. It didn't change the situation, but I was free. With that freedom, I was able to find ways to work through the situation. One way was for us to leave that church and find other ways to serve."

Transform the VERBs

Instead of falling prey to these negative behaviors, make the choice to transform the VERBs into something positive. Be a ***victor***, not a victim. ***Enable*** yourself make your dreams and goals possible,

Strategies for Happiness

through education, developing your inner self, and creating your own dreams and goals instead of feeling entitled and expecting others to provide for you. Claim your personal power through taking full *responsibility* for your life and actions instead of waiting for others to rescue you. Be a *blessing* to those in your life instead of always blaming them for the problems you may experience.

The bottom line is that we all must take full responsibility for our lives and actions. If we mess things up, we can choose to stand up and accept the consequences. If someone does something nasty to us, we can take control, identify positive ways to overcome this and make the decision not to let it control us. We can't control everything that is done to us, but we can control how we will react to it.

As much as I believe in this, I now and then forget. When this happens, I remind myself of the VERBs and take whatever action necessary to transform them again. It's an ongoing process, so don't give up.

> The greatest thing a man can do in this world is to make the most possible out of the stuff that has been given him. This is success, and there is no other.
>
> **Orison Swett Marden**

When we are in the depths of such an event, it's hard to think clearly. That is why it's so important to learn to claim your personal power so that whenever a negative event happens, you don't get enveloped in the pain, but instead, choose what you want it to be and create a meaning that will empower you. Be in control; don't let outer events control or define you.

Personal Power

Claiming our personal power means that we take responsibility for our lives. It's being accountable for our actions. It's responding, instead of reacting. If someone else makes a mess of things and it affects us, we can take control of our response or just react without thinking. It's better to take control and identify positive ways to overcome the situation and make the decision to not let it control us.

Bestow a Blessing

Webster defines a blessing as "the utterance of a wish, request or direction that good should follow, pronounced over a person or an object, or the benefit which follows such utterances."

When you are dealing with others who cause you pain, make a conscious effort to wish them well. Make an effort to think of good things coming their way. Although you need to acknowledge your anger and hurt, don't allow yourself the luxury of hoping that bad things happen to them. Revenge will only hurt you in the end. When we envision good things happening to those that hurt us, we release our pain and the control it has over us.

You Have the Power

It all comes down to the fact that you have the power to choose how your life will be shaped and what attitude you embrace. Will it be one of victimhood, or one filled with joy?

When I was younger, I often took the stance of a victim. It was always someone else's fault that I was upset or angry. I now believe that if I am upset, it's because I choose to allow the circumstance to get the better of me.

Strategies for Happiness

This is especially true in relationships with those I love. One of the most influential factors in my development was my sister Lynn. Though she was 10 years older than me and had moved out to British Columbia when I was 11, I still remember looking up to her, and being inspired in many ways. As a young teenager, she gave me the gift of understanding that no matter what your age, you choose how young you feel.

She is my sister and I love her, but being 10 years older and on the other side of the country made it hard to develop a close bond. Sometimes when we got together, we would get on each other's nerves. We didn't always see eye-to-eye on things, and I sometimes felt resentment toward her.

I always said that Kathleen, our other sister, was our bridge. She helped Lynn and I to connect. When the three of us were together, we had a great time. I remember times when I was with them, laughing so hard I thought I was going to choke.

When Kathleen passed away, our bridge was gone. Though we never spoke about it, I think Lynn may have thought the same thing. Would we drift completely apart, or would we choose to make the effort to find a new connection – our own way of being?

It's amazing how much you lose in life, the opportunities you miss and the life energy you waste because you wallow in self-pity and the need to be right. When you decide to stop being a victim and take responsibility for your attitude instead of blaming others, there is such a glorious freedom.

The event that really made this crystal clear to me was at Kathleen's daughter's wedding. I remember really enjoying myself

Personal Power

that day. It was one of the most delicious and magical days of my life. Sarah, the bride, was stunningly beautiful (always will be), the day sunny and glorious, the wedding, lovely and bittersweet.

In addition to all of these things, I had such a feeling of liberation because I had decided that I was going to just accept Lynn totally, without judgment and without expectation. It wasn't that she had done anything wrong, it was more that I always chose to take everything she did so personally, and often in the wrong way. So I made the choice to open myself to her in a way I never had before. I was not going to let anyone or anything get me down. I claimed my personal power.

The result was that I had one of the most peaceful and powerful weeks of my life. I fully enjoyed seeing Sarah in all her glory. I marveled at the beauty that is my children. I was filled with appreciation and love for my husband, Ken. I was so grateful for all my family and friends. Most of all, I realized just how much I loved and cherished my sister Lynn. I could almost see Kathleen looking down on us, smiling, and saying, "That's right, now you've got it!"

Since then, Lynn and I continue to develop, learn and grow together. We have been able to find that connection and have created a beautiful friendship. I acknowledge Lynn as a marvelous and fascinating person. We have supported each other, taught each other and had a lot of great fun. I find that we are more alike than I ever realized.

Personal power is all about making the choice to be in control and not let other people or events dictate how you will live. Will you be a victim, or a victor?

Give Yourself Permission

We were just about to land in Deer Lake. After much planning and great expectations, my children and I were going to Newfoundland. As I viewed the island from the air, I fell in love. I was filled with joy that I was able to take my children on this trip. We were looking forward to meeting with a friend and having all sorts of exciting adventures. Then a thought crossed my mind, "I don't deserve to be so happy." I almost felt guilty at how happy I felt.

It made me think of the classic movie *A Christmas Carol* starring Alastair Sim as Scrooge. At the end of the movie, Scrooge tells Cratchit that things are going to change. He tells him to go buy more coal to warm up the frigid office. After an amazed Cratchit leaves, Scrooge, sitting at his desk, is so full of glee and merriment.

You can't help but be happy just watching him laughing, giggling, and grinning like crazy. At one point, he gives up trying to work, throws his pen over his shoulder, and exclaims, "I don't deserve to be so happy."

Now if anyone didn't deserve it, it was he. He was such a mean, miserly, selfish old man, but because of his ghostly visitations, he

Give Yourself Permission

learned to change his attitude and ways of thinking. His happiness was not dependent on whether he deserved it or not, but on the fact that he had decided to change his beliefs. Once he did, a whole new world opened up for him.

As I was sitting in that plane, I felt guilty for being so happy – that I didn't deserve it. Then I understood that it had nothing to do with deserving. I had decided I wanted to go, I planned it, I paid for it, and I did it. And yes, I did have a great time.

> The basic fact is that all sentient beings, particularly human beings want happiness and do not want pain and suffering.
>
> ***The Dalai Lama***

Allow yourself to be happy. It's not a matter of whether you deserve it. It's a matter that you choose it. It's as simple as giving yourself permission to be happy and to pursue the life you want. Just say yes to happiness. Allow yourself the freedom to have it in your life.

So often, we feel guilty for feeling happy, or for even wanting to feel happy. We somehow think that it's not right. It's not a matter of being right or wrong. The simple truth is that happiness is there for the taking if you will allow it to be.

You may feel you don't deserve to be happy because your actions and thoughts make you feel unworthy. However, it has nothing to do with what you have done or not done or whether or not you are worthy. You are worthy, just because. It's as simple as that. You exist. Your own personal, wonderful being is as

Strategies for Happiness

worthy as anyone else is to be happy, and you have just as much opportunity to achieve it.

> The first and most important step toward success is the feeling that we can succeed.
>
> ***Nelson Boswell***

On the other hand, your actions may not always be in your best interest or in the best interests of those around you. You may need to take a look at your actions and ensure that they are worthy of you. The fact that you are worthy of happiness is no excuse for behaviour that abuses others or yourself.

If you worry about being worthy of happiness or anything else, or if you are waiting until the magical day arrives that you do something great in order to deserve it, you will wait in vain and waste precious time. We are so conditioned into thinking that we need to be doing something in order to be worthy when, as I have already said, just being is enough.

"But, Donna," you say, "it's so selfish of me to expect or think I am worthy of happiness." Selfish! No way! The best way to serve and help others is to ensure that you are the best you can be, and in being the best, you are able to fully serve and help others. The first step is to learn to love yourself and in order to do that, you need to say yes to the concept.

A common trap is waiting for others to say we are OK. We feel that if others see our value or worth, then maybe it's OK to feel good. This is a big mistake. While it's nice to have others pat us on the back

GIVE YOURSELF PERMISSION

and say nice things about us, it can become addictive, and doesn't give us the solid footing we need. If we give ourselves permission to see and claim our value and worth, then we won't be dependent upon others. We don't need others to tell us that it's okay to be happy. We must come to know that within ourselves.

The first step to doing this is to choose to say "It's okay."

Give Yourself Permission to Feel Bad

While giving yourself permission to be happy is important, there will always be times when you experience negative emotions. Express them, but don't obsess over them.

Give yourself permission to feel what you are authentically feeling. If you feel like crap, you are not authentic if you just smile and say "I am happy" because the truth is, you aren't. The truth is that you will not feel happy every moment of every day.

Instead, express that you are going to give yourself permission to do whatever it takes to develop happiness – to choose to overcome whatever your stumbling blocks are. There is ultimate power in making such a decision. Then move forward by taking the actions that work for you.

Ask yourself questions to help you focus on what you can do to overcome the situation, such as "What is the best way to overcome this situation?" or "What will it take to create happiness in my life?"

For more ideas on questions that can help you get unstuck, read *Optimal Thinking* by Rosalene Glickman.

Strategies for Happiness

Give Yourself Permission to Fail

If we wait until we think we are good enough, we will never get there. Sometimes our attempts fall short. We fall on our face and maybe look a little foolish. Give yourself permission to make these mistakes. Misfires often become wonderful opportunities to learn and grow and are often an opportunity to have a really good laugh.

When you accomplish a task, you get there not because you deserve it or because you are perfect at it but because you conceived the idea, made the plan, and then took action. As a result, you achieved your goal.

Give Yourself Permission to Succeed

We should all take a lesson from my Aunt Lilie who loves to memorize and recite poetry. Even at the age of 92, with most of her sight gone, she still stimulates her brain by learning new poems.

Find a copy of the marvelous poem *Oh, The Places You'll Go!* by the word genius Dr. Seuss and memorize it. It is a marvelous ode about what the future can hold for us, how we have the power to decide what our life is going to be like and a vision for success. It is so positive and down to earth it can really propel you when you are "in a slump." It can help to get you into the mindset of taking control of your life and permitting happiness to happen.

Do not just pin it up so you can look at it now and then, but put your brain to work, and learn the poem by heart. It will exercise your brain, and is a lot of fun, as well as being a fantastic energy builder.

GIVE YOURSELF PERMISSION

When you recite something that has been memorized, it seeps into your pores and becomes part of you, which makes it more meaningful. It is simply a pleasure.

Oh, The Places You'll Go is such a powerful piece that you will find it not only in the children section, but also the business section of bookstores.

After you have this poem under your belt, find more that you can also commit to memory. Build a whole repertoire of poems. Trust me, you will enjoy it.

Give Yourself Permission to be Happy

Since happiness is such a good feeling, people think they have to be good in order to be given permission to feel good. They don't allow themselves the joy of happiness because they feel they don't deserve it.

Brainstorm reasons why it's important to give yourself permission to be happy. Write whatever comes to your mind, and don't stop to think. Force yourself to continue for a full 10 minutes.

After you have finished, create a poster which states the top 5 reasons as follows:

> *I am worthy of happiness and will give myself permission to be happy because . . .*

Place your poster in a prominent location to remind you that from this point onward, you will allow yourself to do whatever it takes to open your life to the Happiness Potential that is waiting to burst forth. You deserve it.

Enough is Enough

People often try to buy their happiness. They think that money will give them a life of leisure, status, security, or power. The question is, can money really buy your happiness? My response is yes . . . and no. As Leo Rosten, the Polish-American writer and humorist once said, "Money can't buy happiness, but neither can poverty."

When is enough enough? Is the pursuit of wealth a bad thing? Not necessarily. Material things can bring us much pleasure and give us the opportunity to enjoy ourselves, but we fool ourselves if we make those "things" the centre of our life. If we do, we will never have enough or be enough.

Sometimes we attempt to buy happiness by giving other people what they want. We endeavour to please them in order for them to like us or give us affection. When we try to purchase happiness by sacrificing our own best interest and integrity, we give up our personal power, which opens us up to grief.

Commercialism works hard to snare you into thinking that you need to own the latest and greatest gizmo. It tries to make us believe that we are entitled to all sorts of stuff. Unnecessary debt often is a result, and is one of the greatest sources of misery in our society.

ENOUGH IS ENOUGH

Many people feel a need "to keep up with the Joneses", so they overspend. The question is, does it really matter if you have all the things they have? Are you going to be any happier? When is enough enough? If you measure happiness by possessions, you will never be authentically happy.

Make the decision that you don't need to keep up with the Joneses. They may not be all that happy anyway. They may have all these gadgets and things, but they now have to take care of and protect them. Imagine what they are paying for insurance alone!

We are influenced by the media and companies that try to trick us into thinking that we need to have all sorts of things in order to be happy. Again I ask, "when is enough enough?" Are you going to let them succeed to seduce you into thinking you are not enough?

> The happy people are those who are producing something; the bored people are those who are consuming much and producing nothing.
>
> **Dean William Ralph**

If you make x number of dollars, you might think that if only you made just a little more, you would be happy. When you get those few extra dollars, do you use them wisely or fall into the trap and just spend them?

You may think, "All I need is a little more money, maybe win the lottery and then I will achieve ultimate happiness." If that "little more" ever does materialize, are you satisfied, or do you still want more? Instead of wishing for a little bit more money to carry

STRATEGIES FOR HAPPINESS

you over the hump, start by learning to live on what you have, and being happy with what you have, now. Distinguish between wants and needs. Money itself is not the problem, it's how you use it. It is not evil, but it's often used for evil things.

> I think there is a serious corruption in the idea sold through advertising that you can attain spiritual peace through lifestyle and the notion of building your happiness from the outside – in by acquiring things, which if you think about it, is the essence of advertising.
>
> **Edward Norton**

Dennis Prager, author of *Happiness is a Serious Problem*, talks about how human nature is insatiable and because of this, we always want more. For example, he talks about how much he likes dessert. He allows himself to have dessert because if he doesn't, it would make him feel deprived. It's human nature that makes him wants to have seconds. However, he knows that if he takes seconds, he will start to eat more then he should and put on weight, which would destroy his health. When his human nature wants to have more, his brain kicks in and he takes control. It's at this point that he decides that one dessert is enough. Anything else will be overkill.

This insatiable nature is not a bad thing if we use it to our advantage. It's what drives us to explore, to learn, to expand the boundaries of the possible. It can lead to wonderful advancement in our society, or lead to mindless materialism. When it comes to our possessions, we need to use discipline and sometimes make the decision that we can be happy with less than we have. Simplification. We need to say enough is enough, whatever that

Enough is Enough

may mean to the individual. Enjoy what we have while being open to the possibilities of what we would like. It does not mean we need to deprive ourselves of items that might give us pleasure; we just need to be wise in what and how we acquire them.

Some people have to have more and more gadgets or the latest and greatest of toys. They have bought into the lie that they have to have these things in order to be happy only to find that after they bought them, they are not only less happy, but also a lot poorer. Some feel they need these things because they fall into the trap of comparing themselves to others. By having many possessions, they are trying to position themselves above the rest of the world by *looking* successful. This gives them a false sense of validation and worthiness.

People often confuse need with want. They fill their lives with things because they think they need them and the things will make them happy and a somebody. Make sure you don't disguise a want as a need. That doesn't mean you can't have any of your wants fulfilled, but don't do it at the expense of your happiness by being burdened with debt and worry.

You need to really examine the reasons for your purchase, and consider if it's going to really be something that will truly enrich your life or simply be a burden. Can you really afford it, or are you just allowing yourself to be talked into it because you think you want it? If you believe it will be worthwhile and you can do it within your means, then go for it. Chances are, if it's something that will really be worthwhile to you, it can wait awhile until you have the cash.

I decided I wanted to buy a car. I didn't really need it because I could use my husband's car most of the time to do shopping and

STRATEGIES FOR HAPPINESS

whatever else I needed to do. However, I got the idea in my head that I wanted one. It was an impulse, and within a week I owned my own car, thanks to a handy, dandy bank loan. I named her Cleo.

I was concerned whether it was wise to borrow for something that, on the surface, seemed like a mega want and not a need. As it turned out, it was a very good decision. Cleo and I have done so much together, and I'm really glad I bought her.

The purchase of Cleo has brought me much happiness. Not because of the fact that I own a car, that it's a pretty red colour, or that it's a specific make or model but because it gives me mobility and opportunity to travel, which is something high on my passion list. It's comfortable, feels good to drive, and gets me from one place to anther safely. I have the enjoyment of remembering the trips I have taken and look forward to the ones I will take. On the surface it may have seemed to be an unnecessary purchase, but for me, it was worth it.

Another time, I went on a trip to Panama with my mother. I had to use my line of credit to pay for it. I don't regret this because otherwise, I wouldn't have been able to go. I didn't want to wait too long to go on this once-in-a-life time opportunity to do something special with my mother, so I figured it was worth the risk. You have to measure the risk and make sure it's worthwhile.

On the other hand, at another point in my life, I tried to start my own business and got into big debt. I realize now that I made an error in judgment, that I didn't spend my money wisely, and that I didn't have a good business idea. I learned from that experience, but paid dearly. It was not a good investment, but the lessons I

ENOUGH IS ENOUGH

learned will eventually make up for it. In my present business, I am taking those lessons to heart, with much better success.

Only you can decide when enough is enough and when it's a worthwhile risk. When you are doing this, make sure to distinguish between wants and needs. You don't need to ignore your wants, just exercise wisdom and common sense.

Another trap is when we spend for our children. We think that if we don't buy stuff for our children – the latest fashions, the coolest toys, the newest computer games, the membership for sports teams – we are not providing and are depriving them of their rights and needs.

When my children were growing up, I didn't have a lot of money to buy them tons of toys and designer clothes, or pay for expensive lessons and memberships. As far as I was concerned, we were not poor. We had what we needed – food, a roof, clothes, as well as many of our wants. We just didn't have money for everything we wanted. At Christmas, they received some nice things, but I didn't spend thousands of dollars on them. I didn't because I couldn't, and I like to think that had I the money to spend, I would not have fallen into the trap of buying them all sorts of unnecessary items.

Now they are on their own, making their own way in the world. They really appreciate what they have. They don't have a sense of entitlement and realize that they have a responsibility to take care of themselves. They are able to make ends meet with a sense of enjoyment. They appreciate their lives and don't expect the world to cater to them.

Strategies for Happiness

Our society does a lot to promote this mentality of entitlement. I knew a single mother who had three children and was on social assistance. At Christmas, the children were given tons of toys from various charities. Many of the things they got were not really appreciated because they were overwhelmed with *stuff*.

Situations like this can breed a sense of entitlement – that the world owes us something. This sense of entitlement will only bring pain, because expectations fall short and there is a temptation to think it's our right to have whatever we want.

It's a hard thing to not have enough, and to struggle for food and shelter. These are clearly needs that have to be met in order to live. True poverty is something that we should do whatever we can to eliminate, and it's worthwhile to help those in need. There is more to poverty than lack of money. It can also be lack of purpose, joy and meaning. Some people with great riches are some of the poorest people in the world.

Contrary to what some might say, there is nothing wrong with the desire to have more than just the basics. In fact, we are all driven by a desire to have a better life, better things, and a better job. The desire for more things or a better quality of life is not the issue. It's when you expect to have more – that feeling that you are entitled to it – when you open yourself to major disappointment. It's not a matter of never achieving your wants, the problem is if you live beyond your present means. Going into debt because of mindless spending or trying to look good is not wise.

There is nothing wrong with being rich. Everyone has the ability and opportunity to acquire abundance and wealth in their

ENOUGH IS ENOUGH

lives. The question is, what do you do with your wealth? Is the pursuit of riches your goal, or is it what you can do with the riches to help yourself and those around you?

I have been asking the question of when is enough enough. The answer is totally up to you. You may be satisfied with just getting by. You may want to go further and acquire abundant wealth so that you can experience all that the world has to offer and share it with others. There is nothing wrong with either view. The point is to be sure that you are pursuing that which will make you the best you can be.

Whatever you do, it's important to be a good money manager. Wealth is a good thing, and can help you to be better able to take care of yourself, do the things you want, and be free and able to help others. If you accumulate wealth, avoid the trap of getting into debt. Buying things on your credit card, making unwise purchases just because you have some spare cash, and getting things just for the sake of getting them is only going to create chaos in your life.

> Capital as such is not evil; it is its wrong use that is evil. Capital in some form or other will always be needed.
>
> **Mohandas K. Gandhi**

Wealth can free you of the burden of having to make a living; you are free to do what you want, when you want. However, if you use your wealth to acquire possessions just for the sake of proving to the world you are somebody or just to look good, you are only setting yourself up for a fall. Wealth, in and of itself, does not make you happy. It's what you do with your wealth that makes the difference.

STRATEGIES FOR HAPPINESS

The key is to learn to live below your means, get out of debt and stay out, and position yourself to be able to do what you want. Make the decision to no longer be burdened with the mentality of living from paycheck to paycheck, and being head over heels in debt.

Make the decision to end your scarcity mentality. No matter what your financial position, be grateful for what you have, and be open for more abundance. Never let the words, "I am poor," ever escape from your lips.

Make Financial Independence Your Goal

In her book, *Stop Working. . . Start Living*, Dianne Nahirny talks about how she decided that she wanted to retire by the age of 32. She did this by buying a house as soon as she could, making wise investments, doing her own repairs, and not having many expenses. She accomplished her goal at 36 and retired at a very young age. So, was she living in a big mansion with lots of servants, dripping with jewels and furs? No. Instead, her income was actually at a level that many would consider to be almost poverty.

> Happiness is not in the mere possession of money; it lies in the joy of achievement, in the thrill of creative effort.
> **Franklin D. Roosevelt**

However, she is very happy. She owns her own house, her expenses are few, she can do what she wants when she wants to, and can afford to travel. Also, she doesn't have to work unless she wants to. That's financial freedom.

Enough is Enough

Get Rid of Clutter

Is it time to simplify your life? One way to do this is to get rid of clutter. Take an inventory of all the things you own. Give your clutter away to others who might really need it. Have a garage sale and give the proceeds to charity. Donate unused items to charities like the Salvation Army or Goodwill.

Designate a "What were You Thinking!?" Trophy

Find an item that screams "What were you thinking?!" Put it in a prominent place to remind you that you don't need to buy just for the sake of buying. When you go to purchase something new, take a look at that item and consider, "Do I really need this new do-dad, or will it become another "What were you thinking?" trophy? Do these things really bring me joy? Why did I buy them? Was it to impress others? Am I trying to buy love and happiness for myself or from others?

If you are considering making a purchase, give yourself a day or two to think about it. Consider if this will add value to your life or become another useless thing. If you are sure, go for it. If not, wait.

After a few days, if you really feel a need for it, the item will still be there. Don't be pressured into buying something just because it's on sale, and if you don't get it now, you will have to pay more or lose it. It may be worth it to pay more and have peace of mind than to buy on impulse and regret it later. Be in control of your life and spending by not allowing salespeople to make you feel you have to buy that item, or there is something wrong with you.

Strategies for Happiness

Create a Spending Plan

Become a conscious spender by creating your own spending plan, instead of a budget. While it's important to be wise with your money, you don't want to have a scarcity mentally. This kind of thinking can make you feel like you are poor, and stuck in poverty. Budgets can help you be careful with your money, but they are too restricting and can foster the poor man thinking.

> The man who does not work for the love of work but only for money is not likely to make money nor find much fun in life.
>
> **Charles Schwab**

A spending plan, while being very similar to a budget, is simply a different way of looking at handling your money. A budget is like being bullied into following the rules, while a spending plan lets me determine how I want to live. I am in control, instead of being controlled by the budget. Instead of limits (budgets) you have boundaries. For more information on how to implement a spending plan, I highly recommend that you read the book *The Complete Cheapskate: How to Get Out of Debt, Stay Out, and Break Free from Money Worries Forever* by Mary Hunt.

Don't Take It Personally

I just got a new job, full of exciting possibilities. Unfortunately, some of my fellow employees were not so happy for me. I couldn't figure out why they were so upset. I didn't do anything that I could see that warranted this reaction. I tried to be helpful and positive. However, the reality was that some individuals seemed to hate me or hold some sort of grudge.

For instance, one person indicated that I had said something to her in the past that hurt her feelings. She had thought I was a *good* person, but now she didn't know. She only liked to be associated with those who she thought were *good* people, and I guess I no longer made the grade.

Wow, what a revelation! I was not a good person, at least according to her. In one fell swoop, I became a horrible person for an act I couldn't even remember doing.

It was around this time that I had the inspiration to write this book. My idea was to research, find practical strategies on achieving happiness, and talk to others about their insights into happiness.

One day I was speaking to a fellow employee about my situation. He gave me some advice, which really turned me around.

STRATEGIES FOR HAPPINESS

He said, "Donna, if those people are upset with you, it's their problem, not yours." These words blew me away. I realized I was allowing the words, thoughts, and perceptions of others to determine my self-worth and value. I have done this all my life.

I could describe myself as being a very accepting person. Though this seems like a good thing, it isn't always so. In my case, as I was growing up, I accepted what others said and thought about me instead of determining my value for myself.

> Rather than wasting energy on what we think we should be doing, we begin to take actions in alignment with who we are.
>
> **John Felitto**

Remember my story about Susan V., the girl that lived up the street from me? She and her friend pulled a wagon blocking my way, called me all sorts of bad things, and wouldn't let me pass. Instead of just crossing the street and ignoring them, I got all upset, turned and went home. On some level I agreed and therefore accepted what they said about me.

When my friend shared with me that I was no longer a good person in her books, I took it very hard. I was sorry for any hurt I may have unknowingly caused. When we come to the realization that we have harmed someone, we need to do whatever is in our power to make restitution and hold ourselves accountable. However, we should not let the event define us.

I knew, deep down, that I was not a bad person, whatever that is, but it still hurt to think that someone else thought it. I took it

Don't Take It Personally

very personally. I had another friend who knew of the struggles I was going through. She lent me a book called *The Four Agreements* by Don Miguel Ruiz. This is a very simple, yet powerful book that helped me to let go of the pain of taking things personally.

Don Miguel Ruiz says that as we grow up, we are taught to believe all sorts of things as true. These ideas involve how we see ourselves and our world. When we accept these concepts and ideas as true, we are in essence agreeing with them. He calls this process "Domestication".

He says, "As children, we didn't have the opportunity to choose our beliefs, but we agreed with the information that was passed to us... As soon as we agree, we *believe* it, and this is called faith. To have faith is to believe unconditionally." The problem is that so often the beliefs we agree to are lies – lies that say that we are unworthy, ugly, or evil. He says that, "If we can see it is our agreements that rule our own life, and we don't like the dream of our life, we need to change the agreements."

In order to facilitate this process, his book outlines four new agreements that we can make with ourselves. The second of these agreements is, "Don't take anything personally." As I read this, I thought to myself, "Yeah right. Sounds nice, but a lot harder to do." The author talks about this agreement by saying,

> *Nothing other people do is because of you... All people live in their own dream, in their own mind; they are in a completely different world from the one we live in... Others are going to have their own opinion according to their belief system, so nothing they think about me is really about me, but it is about them.*

STRATEGIES FOR HAPPINESS

Slowly, it started to sink in and take hold. I chose to make the decision to not take what others said and did personally. I have sometimes forgotten, and fallen victim to the trap, but then I recommit myself to this mindset. The results have been awesome. It has given me such a sense of freedom and power.

> The secret of happiness is this: let your interests be as wide as possible, and let your reactions to the things and persons that interest you be as far as possible friendly rather than hostile.
>
> **Bertrand Russell**

By not allowing yourself to take the actions of others too personally, you are taking control of your life. Honestly look at what is said and done, and if you see that there is no validity to it, disregard it. You know yourself better than anyone else, so you know if something is true, real, and valid. Don't promote a lie by giving it any validity through agreeing to the pain.

Even if the intent was cruel, make sure to examine it to see if there's any truth in it. Then you can decide what needs to be changed and be grateful for the lesson. If there's no truth to it, realize that it will affect you only if you give it permission to do so. Don't let their action define you. Only you can define you.

Visualization

Close your eyes and see the person who has hurt you. Envision yourself telling them in a loving and gentle manner that their view of you is irrelevant and not your reality.

Don't Take It Personally

Now, say to yourself, "I am the creator of my reality and I choose to release this hurt. I forgive. I agree not to take this action personally. I am free and live independent of the good opinion of others." If you sincerely believe your actions have been hurtful and harmful, see yourself asking for forgiveness and see them giving it to you.

Find the Lesson

Though you agree to not taking the action personally, identify at least one lesson you can learn from what has happened and record it in your Appreciation Log. Determine how you can profit from this lesson and take action. Record the actions you have taken and what the results were.

Read *The Four Agreements* by Don Miguel Ruiz

I can't say enough about this book. Buy the book, sit down and read it, today! Don't be put off by some of the mystical sounding language, but study the concepts and open yourself to the simple, common sense, very logical, practical, and powerful message.

This should be a man's attitude: 'Few things will disturb him at all; nothing will disturb him much.'

Thomas Jefferson

Relinquish Rightness

My mother is a very wise woman. She once told me a story about Aunt Ida. She really wasn't my aunt; she was a neighbour who lived across the street. We all called her aunt because she and Mom were very close friends, and our families spent a lot of time together.

Mom shared how one time she went to visit Aunt Ida who was making a cake. While in the process of preparing the icing, she used a spoon to mix the icing. Mom couldn't understand why Ida would use a spoon, when using a knife was so much easier.

She was on the verge of sharing this information with Ida when she stopped herself. It occurred to Mom that even though she preferred to use a knife, it didn't make it wrong to use a spoon.

Are you ever tempted to try to correct others' *mistakes*? We know the best way, and therefore the right way of doing something, and it's our responsibility to tell others how to do it. Or is it?

> The need to be right is the sign of a vulgar mind.
>
> **Albert Camus**

Relinquish Rightness

The need to be right is a major contributor to the problems we face in the world today. We work so hard at trying to prove to everyone what is *right* that we wear ourselves out. Take a look at all the violence and strife in the world. If you look hard enough, you will find that the reason for most of the problems stem from the fact that one person, or group believes in something and wants to dominate another group with that belief. They believe they are right, and no one else has any right to believe otherwise. Often, they use brute force to get their way.

Sometimes, letting other people be right, whether they are or not, disarms them. This encourages open communication allowing them not only to listen to you but perhaps actually hearing you. I think it's more important to do what is right than to always try to prove you are right.

One year I went to Toronto for Christmas. I left my cats in the house with plenty of food and water while I was gone. When I came home, I found that one of my cats had escaped. I think he may have snuck out just before I left, and I didn't see him. The poor thing had been outside all that time.

My upstairs neighbour came out and started berating me for mistreating my cat. She threatened to call the Humane Society and have me charged. My first reaction was to be defensive. I didn't know he was outside. She continued to berate me, and tell me how the poor thing was so hungry, and how she had fed it. She loved animals and hated to see them treated so poorly, etc.

Strategies for Happiness

I continued to defend myself. Then I stopped, looked at her, and said "Thank you." I commended her for her actions, and for helping out. I stopped being defensive and took responsibility for what happened. Immediately she calmed down. She started to talk more softly, and was more willing to listen to me and what I had to say. In the end, I believe she realized it was just an accident and not intentional.

Some people you just can't reason with, no matter what. This is where you have to judge, is this worth fighting for? You may be right, but is this really worth fighting for? If we are honest, we may realize where we may have contributed to the problem. Even if you are right, it's more important to find a solution than to prove to the world that you are right.

> We should listen first and foremost to our own experience... We should stop looking for saviors... Society has not existed for thousands of years because it had a succession of saviors. It's existed because it has institutions and processes through which people can realize their own goals.
>
> **Thomas Sowell**

Often things happen to us that offend us. Have you ever wondered why you may feel offended? Often the feeling of being offended stems from a feeling of insecurity.

For instance, in a situation where someone is trying to sell you something and giving you a hard sell, you might be tempted to be offended. Why should the hard sell upset you so? After all, you don't have to buy it. All you have to say is, "I don't want it." They do not have power over you unless you give it. On some level, people take the hard sell very personally, as if the person is out to get them.

Relinquish Rightness

Clinging tightly to ideas, things, and people severely limits you from enjoying life. I am happiest when I don't have to be right all the time. What a burden it is to have to constantly prove yourself.

Have you ever had this experience, for instance? You get an idea that you think is the most wonderful idea in the world, and you can't wait to share it with others. It is so obvious to you that the idea is wonderful, and if others would agree and go along with it, their lives would be wonderful, as well. It's so frustrating when other people don't immediately agree with you. In fact, for some strange reason, they just turn their back on the idea and won't even give it a chance.

I have had that happen many times. The answer seems so obvious to me. If they would only do what I tell them, their life would be heaven. Then I realized that it was rather arrogant of me to think this way, and sometimes, I am in the wrong.

All people have to find their own way and make their own decisions. Even if it means they may end up suffering. It's their choice – their journey.

Why is it so important to get others to agree with you? When others are agreeable and go along with what we say or want them to do, it could be interpreted as superiority. If you are not strong and secure in yourself, it makes you feel good to get others to go along with you. It makes you feel important.

Whether it is for the good or the bad, others cannot be forced into doing or believing in something just because I think it's a good thing. Maybe the idea is the greatest thing since sliced bread,

STRATEGIES FOR HAPPINESS

but it's not up to me to force it on others. They need to come to it themselves. Besides, I might even be wrong.

It's important to have your opinion and beliefs and to be steadfast. When you are true to what you believe and are open, vulnerable, and willing to share it, you will enrich the world. However, it is also important that whatever your ideas are, you can't force them on others or try to make them adopt your beliefs. Share openly, without condescension or condition, and let them find their own way.

As I write this book, I am excited about sharing what I have learned and the things that have helped me. At the same time, I am constantly reminding myself, "Donna, these are your experiences. Not everyone is going to identity or agree." I decided to just let it go – to share my ideas in the hope that they may inspire others to find their own way, whether through these strategies, or by finding their own strategies. I have the privilege of sharing, but I refuse to preach.

> You have reached the pinnacle of success as soon as you become uninterested in money, compliments, or publicity.
>
> ***Thomas Wolfe***

When I came to this decision, it was such freedom. I no longer have to prove myself to the world. I am free to be, to share, and to no longer carry the burden of the world on my shoulders. Concentrate on developing your inward focus and see how you have contributed. Be your own person – someone who has a strong view, excellent ideas, and is willing to share and contribute, but someone who doesn't need to push themselves or their ideas on

Relinquish Rightness

others in order to prove this. Learn to listen and listen to learn. Resist the urge to fix others.

Develop a Healthy Self-Esteem

The more you are secure with who you are, the less you need to fix others. One way to work on this is to read books and take courses to develop a positive self-image. This may seem obvious, but sometimes we need to be reminded that there is a wealth of knowledge and wisdom from which we can draw and learn.

Here are some programs you might want to consider:

Peak Potentials Training (www.peakpotentials.com)

Peak Potentials' mission is to ". . . educate and inspire people to live in their higher self based in courage, purpose and joy, versus fear, need and obligation." They provide high energy, fun, and life-changing seminars.

Landmark Education (www.landmarkeducation.com)

Landmark Education provides personal development training events "...that are innovative, effective, and immediately relevant. The Landmark Forum, the foundation of all Landmark Education's programs, is designed to bring about a fundamental shift or transformation in what is possible in people's lives."

The Hoffman Institute (www.hoffmaninstitute.org)

The Hoffman Institute has a program called The Hoffman Quadrinity Process which, they say, has produced lasting benefits for more than 50,000 participants all over the world.

Forgive

When I was little, my mother had a friend come over to have lunch with us. This woman had just returned from being a missionary and was very well-known and well-liked in our church.

I remember sitting beside her at the dining-room table. I don't remember the conversation, but I do remember I was babbling away about something, as little children will do (and I was the blabbiest of babblers). At one point, this woman turned to me and said that she had been away for a long time, and that my mother was more interested in what she had to say, than what I had to say. Those were not her exact words, but that is what I remember as the gist of them.

I was young, and maybe didn't understand what she actually said. However, that is what I understood her to say. That is the way my little mind comprehended it. I was crushed and angry. What right did she have to come into my home and say such a mean and selfish thing? And from a missionary at that.

I don't know if my mother heard this comment. She may have been in the kitchen at the time. I like to think that if she had heard it, she would have stuck up for me. I don't remember anything more

Forgive

after that conversation, I just remember being hurt and angry. I never liked that woman after that.

Even years later, when I took my mother to visit her, I remembered that incident with heated anger. I was polite; after all, this was my mother's friend. If I tried to explain it, so long after the fact, who would understand, and who would care?

> The weak can never forgive. Forgiveness is the attribute of the strong.
>
> ***Mahatma Gandhi***

In my mind, I had been truly insulted. At the same time, I also knew that the anger I carried around with me for so many years would prove and produce nothing. I knew that I had to get rid of it, one way or another.

I acknowledged that I had to get rid of it, but I couldn't figure out how. Finally, one night while stuck in traffic, I forced myself to face this pain. I realized that compared to the pain and hurt most people feel in the world, this was nothing, but it was my pain, and it was real.

I couldn't go to this woman and talk to her about it. She had died several years before. Even if she was still alive, how could I explain such a seemingly trivial thing after so long a period of time?

I had a long heart-to-heart with myself. I tried to fully understand the event – why this woman said what she had said. I tried to look on her side of things, as well as acknowledge my side. I considered that maybe she didn't understand what she had done

Strategies for Happiness

– that maybe I misunderstood her words. I worked hard to try and understand both participants without judgment: myself for being over-sensitive and maybe blowing things out of proportion, and her for being insensitive and seemingly selfish.

It didn't really matter if I came to a full understanding of what really happened; I just needed to talk it through. Finally, after much self-talk, I was able to let it go. I forgave her. It didn't matter that she wasn't there to hear the words. It didn't matter that it seemed she had got away with something. It didn't matter if it was real or not. What mattered to me at that point in time was that I was finally free from the pain, the anger, and the victimization I had been carrying around for so many years.

You don't have to face the person that hurt you. Although it would be nice if they owned up to what they did, you can't depend on it happening. Most of the time, people won't remember, or if they did, won't see that it is important. They may even enjoy what they did to you. So, if a face-to-face is not practical or possible, you can manufacture the acknowledgement in your own mind.

> I've had a few arguments with people, but I never carry a grudge. You know why? While you're carrying a grudge, they're out dancing.
>
> **Buddy Hackett**

It's a trap to think that because someone has hurt us, we will never be able to forgive and move beyond it. I know that it's hard – I have had trouble myself – but if you really want to experience the happiness that true freedom brings, then you have to figure out how to let go of the pain through forgiveness.

Forgive

As we go through life, it's inevitable that people are going do things to us that will hurt. When that happens, we have a decision to make. We can be angry, in pain, hurting, holding a grudge, or we make the choice to rise above the need to be right, or the desire to put people in their place, and instead, forgive. Forgiveness is being able to look beyond the event or person that caused the pain. It's choosing to no longer let it have validity or power over you.

People say it takes a long time to forgive. It may seem this way at times, but really, this is a lie we tell ourselves because on some level, we are enjoying our pain. We want the world to say, "Poor little child, it's just too bad." The reality is, we are not poor, but rich and powerful. We can overcome it if we choose to do so.

Forgiveness is something you do primarily for you, and it's in your best self-interest to do so. You don't forgive to make their life better or burden-free. You do it to set yourself free. If you forgive and let them know it, and they appreciate it, even better, but that's not the point.

This may sound selfish, but you have to take care of yourself first if you want to be in the best position possible to help others. If you are burdened with hate, anger, frustration, lust for revenge and bitterness, you cannot be your best, nor help others to a better, richer life. It's hard for people to get their brain wrapped around the idea that when they forgive, it is for themselves and not for the perpetrator of the hurt. As long as you are engulfed with pain, you are their helpless slave.

The first step is to acknowledge your pain, and then make the decision that you want to experience the freedom that forgiveness

Strategies for Happiness

brings. You may not have actually forgiven yet, but by acknowledging your willingness that you really do want to, you are moving in the right direction.

While it's useless to live in the past, it's important to understand why the past can still affect us. Examine your heart and mind. Is it real? Do you have an authentic reason to be upset or are you just holding on to the pain because it is familiar and in that way comforting?

A friend of mine lived through a war that almost destroyed her homeland. What she experienced was a horror most of us have never had to endure. She tells me that it will take her a long time to forgive, if ever. When I tried talking to her about forgiving, she became angry with me and indicated that I was as bad as the people who had abused her.

The last thing I want to do is to trivialize the pain that people suffer. Even so, no matter what degree of hurt people feel, if they don't find resolution, they are just wallowing in their pain and by doing so, allowing the perpetrator to have power over them. It's so hard for people to forgive because by forgiving, it looks like they are giving in to the perpetrator – that they are letting him/her get away with it.

It's actually the other way around. Through forgiveness, you free yourself from the bondage of pain and allow yourself to find joy. For myself, I would rather forgive and be free than to hold on to the pain in order to prove to the world that I am right. Those who refuse to forgive may feel satisfaction in the thought that maybe the person or persons that hurt them are suffering because they are not being forgiven. In reality, this is most likely not the case.

FORGIVE

I once knew a man who had treated me badly. His presence filled me with loathing and anger. One night, I had to go to a dinner party where he was also a guest. I remember how I was seething with anger and hate, just at the sight of him. Then something snapped within me. I realized that this anger – this hatred – was killing me, and that what he did and how he acted affected me only if I allowed it.

All of a sudden, I wanted desperately to get rid of my anger, and my pain. I realized the only way I could do that was to forgive him. That didn't make what he did right, but it would make my life right again. That is what mattered to me. I wanted to be free from this burden.

> If we really want to love we must learn how to forgive.
> **Mother Teresa**

In the whole scheme of things, his actions were irrelevant. What was relevant to me was how I felt, and how I lived. I could go through my life being miserable and angry, filled with hurt – or I could enjoy being emotionally free. I realized in that moment that the only way to stop the pain was to forgive – fully, openly, without strings attached.

Did it happen at that moment? No. What did happen was that in that moment, I realized what I had to do, and vowed to do it. Not for him, but for me. Did it make me some sort of saint? No way! I just didn't want him to have power over me anymore. That point of recognition – of awareness that I needed to forgive – was pivotal. I took the first steps toward doing it, and that in itself was a great

Strategies for Happiness

relief. Learning to forgive may be a challenge, but it gives much freedom.

When someone has wronged you, and you hold a grudge towards him or her, they continue to hold power over you. Whether they realize it or not, whether they even care, they will continue to hold power over you until you let it go.

I don't suggest that someone should just get away with it because you forgive. Take whatever action you think is necessary in the context of the situation, but remember that your happiness is more important than proving to the world that you were right and they were wrong.

> Pain is inevitable. Suffering is optional.
>
> **Zen Aphorism**

Does that mean I am always able to forgive? No, at least not right away. The difference is that now I know the freedom forgiveness gives me. I prefer freedom to bondage, so if I find myself holding a grudge, I try to create a reason to push me to do it.

Sometimes when you are angry with people, and when it's hard to forgive, it may be because on some level, you refuse to acknowledge your responsibility in the situation. You hide behind the hurt and say, "It's all their fault, they did this to me." Stop for a moment to consider that maybe in some way you are contributing to the situation. That still doesn't make their behaviour right but you need to be open to the possibility that your actions are adding to the problem.

Forgive

When I was about 10, I was hit by a car while walking my bike over a crosswalk. The car in the first lane stopped, but the car in the second lane didn't see me and hit me in the behind. I guess you could say I got rear-ended.

An ambulance was called and I was rushed to the hospital. When I was in the hospital, I was visited by a police officer. He didn't get angry at me, and he didn't blame me for what happened, but he did ask me that when I walked across the cross walk, did I try and look to see if it was okay to cross? I was in the right. It wasn't my fault, but was I actively aware of my surroundings? Was there any way that I could have prevented what happened?

Being Responsible

This question made a deep impression on me, and now, when in situations of conflict, I do my best to be aware of my place in the scheme of things, and how my actions can affect the situation, whether I am in the right or the wrong.

It comes back to being accountable for your actions. Events may happen that are outside your control, but you are still accountable for how you respond to them. If you were abused as a child, you might grow up carrying a burden of shame, guilt and anger. There may be good reason to be angry.

Accountability means looking at the whole picture and making the decision to change your response to something that is in your best interest. Hatred, unresolved anger, and suffering will not serve you. By being accountable, you are saying that you want to take control of your life and will not be manipulated.

STRATEGIES FOR HAPPINESS

Forgiveness is a response that gives you freedom, which will make you happy. Forgiveness is taking back your personal power. It seems so hard to do because we think we are giving in when we are really showing strength. It's saying to whoever hurt you, "You no longer have control over me. I am no longer your slave. I am stronger than you."

> We all know people who say: "It's the principle of the matter" to justify sustaining toxic emotions for years. As they hold onto their anger or hurt, they bleed away their energy reserves, often ending up bitter and depressed.
>
> **Doc Childre and Howard Martin**

We often feel that we have the right to be bitter or angry. However, we pay a heavy price for claiming that right. On the other hand, freedom is such an exquisite feeling of lightness and joy as well as a wonderful serge of power. By being free, you have much more control over your life.

People don't want to forgive because they want to prove to the world that they are right. If they forgive, it may be perceived that they are somehow wrong. This is both foolish and childish. If you know in your heart that you are right and still can find the strength to forgive, what does it matter what others, even the perpetrator, think? By forgiving, you are breaking that chain.

Forgiveness is not a get-out-of-jail card. There is a difference between forgiving and holding people accountable for their actions. What you need to concentrate on is not whether they get their comeuppance, but to ask yourself "What is the best thing for me to do?

FORGIVE

What is going to free me to be the best I can be and feel fulfilled and happy?" The answer to that is to forgive and move on.

Those that hurt you need to face the consequences of their actions. That could be as simple as losing your friendship or as serious as going to jail. Whatever it is, don't feel that because you forgive, they get off without any repercussions, but don't fall into the trap of looking for and enjoying revenge. That only brings you to their level.

Anger is a normal reaction, and one that shouldn't be ignored. It often is a signal we need to heed. It is important that we stop and listen to the message it has for us. When anger is not dealt with properly, it can turn inward and grow into resentment and bitterness often leading to depression. By forgiving, we can release the anger before it can become harmful.

It is also a trap to feel that the perpetrator should first acknowledge what they did and ask for forgiveness, before we, in our largess will condescend to consider doing it. It doesn't work that way. You can't wait for the other person to acknowledge what he/she has done. People often don't know that they have done anything to you, or may not even care. They may even get a kick out of it.

The power of forgiveness is not dependent on interaction with the person that has hurt you, but is completely in your power and control. When you believe that giving your forgiveness is dependent on the other person's admission of guilt, you are locked in a vicious circle of pain that will not be resolved.

You can't expect those that hurt you to come and ask for forgiveness. If you wait until that happens, most of the time you

Strategies for Happiness

will remain in pain. Why wait? Remember, it's your best self interest to forgive. That person may not be in your life anymore. They may have moved away, or died. If you feel the need to wait until they ask for forgiveness, you are doomed. The perpetrator is not in need of forgiveness so much as you are in need to forgive.

I once heard a woman speak about how she was able to forgive the individual that brutally murdered her child. I was impressed that this person could have such strength in the face of this horrible event. Yet, I think she was also very wise. The murderer should still be punished, but because she was able to forgive, she was no longer in his power.

On the other hand, I once spoke to a man who said if anyone ever hurt one of his daughters, he would kill the person. He figured that as long as his wife was there to take care of their other daughter, he would be willing to go to jail for killing whoever harmed his child.

> Always forgive your enemies; nothing annoys them so much.
> **Oscar Wilde**

I could not help but feel that this would be one of the most selfish acts anyone could do. He takes revenge, kills a person, goes to jail and now, not only has a child lost her sister, but also her father. A woman not only loses her daughter, but also her husband. She now has to carry on by herself to care for their child. She no longer has his income, so she has to work more, and their child has to do without.

Now, if this person were to move beyond the pain, forgive the perpetrator (remember, I didn't say let them get away with it) and

FORGIVE

heal, he would be there to help his wife and child through it all. He could use this experience to help others.

The actual process that you go through in order to obtain the peace that comes with forgiving is a very individual thing. Be open and honest that you have felt pain. Life can be very messy sometimes and denial is not going to make it any better. Instead of denial, allow yourself to feel the pain, and you will work through it and heal faster.

Take a look at what hurt you and examine all sides of the situation. Put yourself in the position of the individual who hurt you and try and understand where he/she is coming from. Again, understanding is not agreeing.

The Three People to Forgive

There are three people you need to forgive. First of all your parents or whoever was your major caregiver growing up. These people were only human, with their own warts and wrinkles, their own demons and damage from their past. They did the best they could with what they had. Even if they didn't do their best and were just downright nasty, forgive them so they will no longer have power over you.

Secondly, forgive the other people in your life that may not have been the best of friends, who used you or abused you. Examine the reason you are hurt   Put yourself in their shoes. Be open and honest and examine all sides of the situation.

Then last and most important, forgive yourself. Give yourself a break. Allow that you are human and make mistakes. Love yourself enough to let go of the pain.

STRATEGIES FOR HAPPINESS

Heal the Wound

Unless you make the effort to forgive you will not heal, period. As long as you hold a grudge, you will be in pain. Pain in the body is a sign that something is wrong. Something needs to be attended to.

Imagine that someone hit you and made you bleed. If you waited until that person asked for forgiveness before you took care of the wound, it would get infected and would fester. The smart thing would be to get it looked after immediately. You would clean the wound, bandage it up, and keep it clean. If it were bad enough, you would go and see a doctor or health care provider, get it stitched, and put ointment on it. You would do everything in your power to make sure that the wound healed properly.

> Yesterday is gone. Tomorrow has not yet come. We have only today. Let us begin.
>
> **Mother Teresa**

Why? First of all, because you don't want to die. Secondly, because a treated wound feels better – a healed wound even better. If a wound is taken care of, it will heal faster and there will be less chance of a scar or infection. Soon, you will be back on your feet, out there enjoying life again. The longer you leave the wound full of poison and dirt, the closer you get to death, and you will always be in pain.

There is little difference between physical pain or holding a grudge. If someone hurts you, do whatever it takes to move towards healing. Bitterness will never heal a soul's wound – only make it fester and die.

FORGIVE

Nine Steps to Forgiveness

The website *www.learningtoforgive.com* has the following steps, developed by Dr. Frederic Luskin, which are designed to help you in your effort to forgive.

1. Know exactly how you feel about what happened and be able to articulate what about the situation is not OK. Then, tell a trusted couple of people about your experience.

2. Make a commitment to yourself to do what you have to do to feel better. Forgiveness is for you and not for anyone else.

3. Forgiveness does not necessarily mean reconciliation with the person that hurt you, or condoning of their action. What you are after is to find peace. Forgiveness can be defined as the "peace and understanding that come from blaming that which has hurt you less, taking the life experience less personally, and changing your grievance story."

4. Get the right perspective on what is happening. Recognize that your primary distress is coming from the hurt feelings, thoughts and physical upset you are suffering now, not what offended you or hurt you two minutes – or ten years – ago. Forgiveness helps to heal those hurt feelings.

5. At the moment you feel upset, practice a simple stress management technique to soothe your body's flight or fight response.

6. Give up expecting things from other people, or your life, that they do not choose to give you. Recognize the "unenforceable rules" you have for your health or how you or

STRATEGIES FOR HAPPINESS

other people must behave. Remind yourself that you can hope for health, love, peace, and prosperity and work hard to get them.

7. Put your energy into looking for another way to get your positive goals met than through the experience that has hurt you. Instead of mentally replaying your hurt, seek out new ways to get what you want.

8. Remember that a life well-lived is your best revenge. Instead of focusing on your wounded feelings, and thereby giving the person who caused you pain power over you, learn to look for the love, beauty and kindness around you. Forgiveness is about personal power.

9. Amend your grievance story to remind you of the heroic choice to forgive.

Dr. Luskin says,

The practice of forgiveness has been shown to reduce anger, hurt depression and stress, and leads to greater feelings of hope, peace, compassion, and self confidence. Practicing forgiveness leads to healthy relationships as well as physical health. It also influences our attitude, which opens the heart to kindness, beauty, and love.

You have the full right to carry the burden of the pain of your past if you choose to. But, why would you want to? Have you ever had to carry something heavy for a long while – a sack of potatoes, a computer monitor, a baby? When you put it down, you feel such a release and lightness. You can stretch and move and relax. You say

Forgive

to yourself, "Boy, is that heavy or what? Does it ever feel good to put it down." Forgiveness is like that. You feel light. You feel free.

Sometimes, You Need to be Forgiven

Forgiveness goes both ways. Sometimes we are the ones who disrespect and violate other. This reflects badly on our character, and will ultimately hurt us. As much as each individual is responsible for their own choices in how they may respond to negative events, if we have been instrumental in their pain, then it is in our best interest to seek forgiveness and find ways to resolve the issue.

By seeking forgiveness, we acknowledge that we have been disrespectful, making them understand that they are being heard and taken seriously. This awareness can helps in the healing.

Once you have asked for forgiveness, you need to let it go. They may forgive, or they may not. If they do forgive, thank them for their gift. If not, accept it. You cannot force it.

Do whatever you can to resolve your differences. However, if they refuse to participate by forgiving, don't allow yourself to be overwhelmed with guilt. You have done your best to resolve it, and if they choose to continue in the pain, that is their choice. Learn from the situation, and move on.

Forgiveness, whether we give it, or seek it, is vital in the development of your happiness potential. Forgiveness is healing. Forgiveness is empowerment. Forgiveness is freedom.

Pursue Your Passion

Kathleen said to me, "Lynn and I are planning to go to Greece in 2001 to celebrate that I am fifty. Do you want to join us?" In that split second, I said yes. I didn't know how I was going to do it or how I was going to pay for it, but I knew that I was going to go. A chance to go on such a trip with my sisters was a once-in-a-lifetime opportunity.

Turning fifty is a special time in one's life. For some, it's a time of sadness because their life is half over. For others, it's a time to look back and enjoy.

For Kathleen, it was even more special. She had just battled cancer, which made us all aware of how precious and fleeting life is. One might live to be 100 or be gone the next day. You need to enjoy life to its fullest every moment of the day and not waste a precious moment. So, when she asked me to join her and Lynn, I was on board.

The next year, we were on a plane bound for Greece. We had a very special and wonderful time. We explored the wonders of Athens, relaxed on the beaches of Santorini, and immersed ourselves in the history of Rhodes.

Pursue Your Passion

The trip almost didn't happen. A few months before we left, Kathleen's cancer had returned – this time in her lungs. She had to go through chemo and radiation treatments, lost her hair, and couldn't walk very far without gasping for breath.

I was visiting her one day, and we went out for lunch not far from her home. Walking home, we had to stop many times so she could catch her breath. On one such stop, she confessed to me that she didn't know if she would be able to make the trip to Greece. She didn't know if she was going to be up to it.

This filled me with sadness, not just because I wanted so much to go, but because I wanted to have this special time with her, and I knew deep down that she wasn't going to be with me much longer.

What Are You Passionate About?

Kathleen had many dreams – many things she wanted to do with her life. She had accomplished many of them, but she had put many aside to take care of others. There would always be time later, or so she thought. Now the reality was coming home that she didn't have much time left to achieve some of her dreams.

One of those dreams was to go to Greece. Being an artist, she wanted to experience the beauty and the art that was Greece. She always had a dream to someday see the famous "Porch of the Maidens", the beautiful female statues that doubled as pillars at the Acropolis in Athens.

Some might have given up and said "What's the use?!" but not Kathleen. She had one more radiation treatment, which really made a difference. On the surface, she seemed almost as

Strategies for Happiness

good as new. Underneath, however, the cancer was still there, slowly taking over her body.

So we were able to go to Greece. I met them on the plane as it stopped in Montreal. I remember walking down the isle toward our seats where they were waiting for me, smiling and giggling like gleeful children, all excited about our adventure. I was struck with Kathleen's hair, which was very short – a reminder of what she had been going through. It had just started growing in again after her treatments, so she didn't have to wear a wig.

We had a wonderful time together. We knew our time together was limited, so we really made the most of it. I treasure the special moments when Kathleen and I had some profound heart-to-hearts.

One particular marvelous day, I decided to go off on my own. I left my sisters to lounge on the beach, hopped on a local bus, and headed into Fira, the capital of Santorini. I had an amazing day. I felt so utterly free, and filled with joy and bliss. It was a time of feeling so totally at one with my life. There was such passion in that moment – an intensity that I believe we are meant to feel – our true essence. I look at that day – that state of mind – and believe that it is an example of the way we all can be – that it is the purpose for our existence. The lesson I learned that day is that we should do whatever it takes to find what we are truly passionate about – what really fills us with authentic joy. **We should never settle for anything less**!

After this wonderful day, I wandered back to the hotel. I was walking up the road towards the hotel when I saw two figures at a table in front of our hotel. It was Lynn and Kathleen, just returned from their own adventure. They somehow knew I was coming,

Pursue Your Passion

because they had a cup of tea waiting for me. What a way to cap off one of the most spectacular days of my life – sitting quietly in the dark, drinking tea and sharing our stories of the day. Sisters are truly a special gift.

Kathleen confessed to me later, that even though she had enjoyed the day, she was worried about me, off on my own. She was always looking out for me. When I confessed to being nervous about swimming because of sharks, she told me not to worry. She

Kathleen always dreamed of going to the Acropolis of Athens in Greece to stand among the famous "Porch of the Maidens," the six draped female figures, otherwise known as caryatids, which also act as supporting columns.

Strategies for Happiness

said, she wouldn't swim in waters where there was sharks. I think she just said that to reassure me, because I know there were sharks somewhere, just waiting for me. It must have worked though, because we didn't see any.

The cancer was always there. Even though she was feeling much better, she was still weak, short of breath, and had a constant pain in her chest. She tried her best to not let it affect our time together, but it was still there, waiting.

> We ourselves feel that what we are doing is just a drop in the ocean, but the ocean would be less because of that missing drop.
>
> **Mother Teresa**

The day we visited Lyndos on the island of Rhodes, it was so hot that I literally tore my clothes off to jump into the cool, clear, marvelous water of the Mediterranean Sea (don't worry, I had my bathing suit on underneath). Kathleen was already in the water and saw me coming. She knew by the look in my eye what I was planning to do.

We had come to Lyndos by boat, which was anchored on the large dock to the right. When coming into the port, I noticed a number of caves along the coast, on the other side of the dock. I had a yen to go and visit the caves and thought it would be fun to swim to them. She understood right away where I was headed and decided to go with me, again to keep a sisterly eye on me.

Though she was weak, she loved to swim, and the lovely saltwater made it easy, so off we went to explore the caves. It was the most lovely swim of my life with the beautiful blue sky and the

Pursue Your Passion

buoyant crystal clear water where you could see all the way to the bottom. I was amazed at being able to clearly see the huge anchor attached to the thick cable that kept our ship docked and waiting for us. We got to the caves, explored, enjoyed, and found a way to walk back to the others. It was such a special time with Kathleen.

The last night we were in Greece, we went out for one last dinner in the Old City in Rhodestown. After dinner, Kathleen and I left Lynn to do her own thing and decided to go into the Market to buy something special to commemorate our trip.

The Old Town of Rhodes is a mediaeval city on Rhodes, with a large walled moat surrounding it. The moat around the city was a magnificent passageway, and at night it was dark and mysterious. I will always remember that walk as we made our way to the market. It really was like stepping back in time.

We walked through the market and looked over the many items being offered to us. Finally we found just the right thing. Kathleen and I each bought a small metallic horse statue, their hoofs stamping haughtily as only a Grecian horse can. I have both of them proudly displayed on my piano today.

The September after we returned home, the cancer took a turn for the worst. She had to stop working and wasn't able to travel anymore. In November, she turned 51. The following July, she passed away.

Don't Wait for Your Ship to Come In

What does all of this have to do with passion? Kathleen was a passionate person. She loved her life, and did what she could to get

STRATEGIES FOR HAPPINESS

the most out of it. She had overcome many struggles, and did so with grace and passion. She was only 51 when she died.

I want this story to wake you up. What are you doing with your life? Are you living it to the fullest? Are you waiting for more time, the right time or enough money before you start to live? Are you wasting even a precious moment of your day on self-pity, anger, frustration, envy, or anything else that would take away from your joy?

Are you stuck in the trap – the lie that life is just to be endured, or that mediocrity is inevitable?

While in Santorini, we went on a cruise that took us to a sulfur spring that was fed by an active volcano. It was said that these springs had mystical healing powers.

> Do not let your fire go out, spark by irreplaceable spark, in the hopeless swamps of the approximate, the not-quite, the not-yet, the not-at-all. Do not let the hero in your soul perish, in lonely frustration for the life you deserved, but have never been able to reach. Check your road and the nature of your battle. The world you desired can be won. It exists, it is real, it is possible, it is yours.
>
> **Ayn Rand**

Kathleen and I both jumped into the water with great gusto. We swam the short distance to the sulfur pools. The closer you got, the nastier the water tasted, as the sulfur mixed with the already acrid taste of salt. Finally we reached the spring, and walked in as close as we could get. The water was warm, heated by the volcano, just a short distance away. It was very muddy. We covered ourselves with

Pursue Your Passion

the mud. What a sight we were! At one point, she stood up, and put her hands in the air, and proclaimed, "I'm healed!" We both roared with laughter.

Though cancer would eventually take her life, it didn't stop her from living. Learn the lesson of her life. Don't wait for your ship to come in; jump in the water and swim into your passion.

Find out what you really love to do and then take action to make it happen. That way, whatever you do, it won't feel like work. When people are trying to find out what to do with their lives, they often ask questions like "How much money can I make?" "What kind of demand is there for this job?" "What kind of advancement can I expect?"

People are taught to believe that if they work hard, someday it will all pay off, and they will be able to retire and have some fun. With being caught up in the trap of retirement and sticking with a job that is no fun and of no interest, they feel they can't leave because of all their seniority. Leaving too soon will mean losing their retirement package. It's such a waste of potential and passion.

My parents loved to travel, and they figured once my father retired, they could spend the rest of their lives traveling. Less then a year after retirement, it was found that my father had a brain tumor. After a year of suffering, he finally passed away.

Though my father did not live to achieve his dream in retirement, he did have a wonderful life. He enjoyed being married the love of his life, was a loving father to three adoring daughters, was able to travel and see much of the world, and above all, just enjoyed having fun. Yes, he was looking forward to his retirement so he could do more of it, but didn't wait until it was too late.

STRATEGIES FOR HAPPINESS

Unfortunately, there are so many people that live their life in the future and miss out on really living. They say, "One day, when this or that happens, then I will be happy." I know, I still find myself saying it.

When we are young, we have so many dreams and aspirations. There is so much we want to do, to experience, and to enjoy. As we go through life, if we are not careful, we can let the events of our lives snuff out our spark, putting out our fire. We put off what we really want because we feel it's just not time yet.

> Don't ask yourself what the world needs; ask yourself what makes you come alive. And then go and do that. Because what the world needs is people who have come alive.
>
> **Chinese proverb**

So ask yourself, what really makes you excited? What gets your heart pumping with joy? The world can use people who are truly alive. Find out what you really love to do, and then find the way to make it happen.

Ask yourself, if you had all the money in the world, all the time, and you knew that you were going to die in six months, what would you do with your life? It is really a hard question to answer, I know, but it does help you to focus in on what is really important to you.

Only you know what your dreams are – what you are passionate about. Your passion is something you would be willing to do even if you didn't get paid. Be honest. What do you really want to do? Don't worry about what others think or want for you. It's not their life, it's yours.

Pursue Your Passion

Maybe your passion is sharing joy with others through music or writing. Maybe your passion is expressing the pleasure of colour and light through stained glass creations or painting. It could be helping people better their lives through goods and services you provide or the opportunity to heal others mentally or physically. Whatever your passion, it needs to be expressed, and by doing so, you will touch the world.

Your passion needs to be healthy and one that contributes to your well being, with positive consequences. Happiness is fueled by purpose, which is fueled by passion. Passion is energy.

It's a fact. You have the same amount of time in your day as anyone else. Therefore, make sure to not waste a minute of it living according to someone else's plan. Be true to who you are and what you want from your life, not what others want you to do. It's your life, your goal, your passion that is the only thing of importance in your life. Even if the world looks on your choices and the result as foolish, it's still your choice and that is something to celebrate. Don't allow others to make those choices for you.

I have always been interested in music, though was never formally trained. I decided to go to college and major in Music. I looked forward to learning how to read music properly, how to direct choirs, play the piano, sing in a choir, etc.

At that time, we had various activities going on in our church. Someone had formed a choir of the young people, and we tried to put together a Christian rock band. There was no real leadership in the group, and we didn't really know what we were doing, but we had fun.

STRATEGIES FOR HAPPINESS

I got the idea that when I went to college, I might be able to help the group. I was very excited about learning all I could about music and using these skills to help out. In my excitement, I went a little overboard in anticipation of how I would lead the band.

I guess I got a little too big for my britches because one day the youth leader of the church took me aside to have a little chat. I think my attitude bugged him, and he felt it that he needed to set me straight and put me in my place. Whatever the reason, he basically didn't believe in me or my dream. His message to me basically was "Don't pursue the music program. You don't have what it takes."

> The aim of life is to live and to live means to be aware – joyously, drunkenly, serenely, divinely aware.
>
> **Henry Miller**

In his mind, he thought I had bitten off more than I could chew and thought to spare me the pain of failing. However, if we have a goal, an idea we want to pursue, we should not allow others to dissuade us. While you should be open to what others have to say – because there is often wisdom in their words – in the end, you need to be aware of your own needs and do what is best for you. After all, you are the one that has to live with the consequences.

As it turned out, I had already decided that the music program was not for me and had changed to another major. I made that decision not because he told me to but because I had decided I wanted to go in a different direction. When college started, I saw what the course

Pursue Your Passion

entailed, I knew that I had made the right decision – my decision, my choice.

Don't let anyone talk you out of your dream. No matter how impossible it seems to the world, if it's what you really want, do whatever it takes to achieve it. If you do achieve that specific dream, great. Otherwise, along the journey you might find it's not what you really want, and you can change your direction toward what you now really want. It is all a journey, but you will not get anywhere if you don't attempt to start.

Don't stop, no matter what others say, unless you realize it's what you want to do. Be open to changing your mind if you realize the direction you have taken is not where you want to go. There is nothing wrong with re-thinking your goals.

As you pursue your passions, you may have times that you fall flat on your face. That's okay; at least you tried. Always allow yourself the freedom to consider the possibilities. You won't know unless you attempt it and find out the lessons it can bring you. Otherwise, you will always wonder what might have been.

You Can Always Learn What You Need to Know

Don't let your lack of knowledge stop you from pursuing your passions. If it is your passion, you can always learn what you need to know. It's not lack of knowledge that stops people from achieving their dreams; it's lack of determination. If there is something you are truly passionate about, the energy to persevere will be there. You won't have to force yourself.

STRATEGIES FOR HAPPINESS

One of my passions was to become a professional speaker. While I realize that there are many others who have more experience and ability than me, I can always develop and learn the needed skills to achieve this goal. By doing this, I have learned so many fantastic lessons and have had a blast in the process.

After doing one of my Strategies for Happiness workshops, a participant came up to me and thanked me for my presentation. She said, "It was very motivational." She paused, and then added, "It was very life-changing motivation." That filled me with such joy to know I had touched someone – maybe even changed a life.

So find your passion and don't let people stop you. Be open to what others have to say but always decide what is right for you – what resonates with your being. Pursue your passion and then no matter what happens in your life, it will be full. If you find and live your passions, the world will be a richer place for everyone, including yourself. Remember the lesson of Kathleen.

Often people attempt to live their lives backwards; they try to have more things, or more money, in order to do more of what they want, so they will be happier. The way it actually works is the reverse. You must first be who you really are, then do what you need to do, in order to have what you want.

Margaret Young

Overcome the Judge

There is a microwave in the kitchen of one of my clients that everyone can use. It sometimes gets dirty from use. Someone, in frustration, put up a sarcastic note saying, "Don't use it if you don't know how to clean it."

I went to use it one day to find it dirty. I know that I didn't cause the dirt, but I decided to clean it. I could just imagine the person who put up the note frothing and fuming about whoever didn't clean up after themselves.

For myself, I was of a mind that what's done is done. I am not going to judge the person that made the mess. I didn't want to invest my time and energy contemplating what kind of person would do such a thing.

I am happiest when I'm not being judgmental. Judging others is a burden; it weighs you down with a feeling of what is right and wrong, namely I am right and you are wrong. If you don't agree with me that you are wrong, you annoy me. That's why road rage is all the rage.

Being judgmental is the source of much of the pain in the world. We judge things right or wrong, good or bad, weak or strong. How do we know that we have what it takes to make a true

Strategies for Happiness

judgment on a situation? All we have is our perception of the world and what we have learned. There are some people in this world who have made a judgment that we in the West are evil, and should be wiped out. Then there are those here in the West who believe they have cornered the truth and that the terrorists are pure evil.

> Do not condemn the judgment of another because it differs from your own. You may both be wrong.
>
> **Unknown**

We often tend to judge others as good or bad depending on whether or not they agree or disagree with our views and thoughts. If you don't agree with me, there is something wrong with you. We are supposed to be living in a society where free speech and free thought are promoted, but if you disagree with me, watch out. What ever happened to agreeing to disagree?

If you have hurt me, you are bad. I am a nicer person than you are. You did something wrong twenty years ago, so you are evil. Yesterday, I helped a little old lady across the street, so I am better than you are.

If judging others isn't bad enough, we are constantly judging ourselves as well. Am I dressed right? Do I have enough money? I'm better than you? I'm a bad boy/girl?

Stop it! Whenever we put ourselves above or below someone, we are putting ourselves in danger of judgment. Stop comparing and start concentrating on being the best you can be – not being better or worse than the others around you. Stop putting yourself down because so and so is a bit better at some task than you are, or

OVERCOME THE JUDGE

they have had more opportunities than you have, or have many of the things you want. So what?

Concentrate on yourself, in the present, in the moment. Find the thing that makes you tick, that makes the *best you* come alive. If it requires that you compare yourself or judge yourself on some sort of man-made standard, then you have missed the point. If you have to put someone else down in order to make yourself feel good, then there is something faulty in your thinking.

Learning to stop judging either yourself or those around you frees you up to attain the number one goal of your life – learning to love yourself fully and unconditionally. Judgments are a major block to this goal. Free and abundant love will not live in the same area as judgments.

There is a time and a place to use our judgment, as long as it is used wisely and is in the best interest of all, not as evidence that your way of thinking is better than that of others. A judge is supposed to be impartial, not carried by the emotions of the event. They are supposed to look at the facts and determine, without prejudice, what is the best course of action.

If we are standing before a judge in a court of law, we hope the judge will be fair in making his/her judgment. In this case, it's not a matter of emotion but a matter of what is the best course of action for the situation. In reality, judges are human and have been known to let their personal views cloud their decisions. The principle still remains that there are times we need to assess the situation and decide what to do about it. This is valid and not a problem. The problem is when we judge in such a way as to determine other peoples' worth.

Strategies for Happiness

Of course, it is then up to the other person to determine whether or not they are going to accept your view of them and, if they are strong and smart, they will know that your view of them does not determine who they are. On the other hand, what does it say about you and your character?

If you put someone else down, you are trying to prove you are a better person than they are. It's arrogant of you to do so. Arrogance says that you are insecure about who you are because you need to make someone else look bad in order to make yourself look good. It's a "look at me" mentality.

Comparing yourself in a negative way is also a judgment and a way to get the focus on yourself. You want the world to see you in all your supposed insignificance, to point out to the world that you know you are bad before they can do it for you. If you point out your weakness before they do, then somehow you feel you are okay. It's still a "look at me" mentality.

There are times when we need to made decisions about our life. We say that we need to use our best judgment to determine what to do. We take all things into consideration, determine the best course of action, and then decide to move forward. This is valid and necessary.

This is different from placing judgment on others' worth. Destructive judgment is all about comparisons. I am a better person because I have more money than you, I am prettier than you, I have a better education than you . . . and the list goes on.

There is nothing wrong with enjoying abundance and wealth, appreciating the finer aspects of your mind or body, or sharing your knowledge and talents with others. However, when you start

OVERCOME THE JUDGE

to declare that you are somehow better or more worthy than others because you possess certain abilities or possessions, you are only going to end up hurting yourself.

> Whoever undertakes to set himself up as judge in the field of truth and knowledge is shipwrecked by the laughter of the Gods.
> **Albert Einstein**

You are not a mind reader and cannot know all and see all as to why people act the way they do. For instance, I am amazed when I hear people talk about other people's driving habits. I agree that sometimes people show poor judgment when driving and have done some careless things. However, by the way people talk, you would think that other drivers are the lowest of criminals and should be locked away without a trial.

Just because people make mistakes while driving doesn't mean they are like that all the time or that they go home and beat up their family. We don't know what is going on inside the head of people at the time they do certain actions. Who are we to judge them as bad?

Again let me state, as I have done many times before, that all people need to be held accountable for their actions, but to determine that they are bad just because you don't like what they did is not in your best interest.

While visiting a community I used to live in, I walked past two women and said, "Hi." Later, I was informed by another resident that the women I passed did not hear me as I went by. One of these ladies thought that I had purposely snubbed her.

STRATEGIES FOR HAPPINESS

After that, she would not talk to me, or return my call. She didn't want to talk to me or have anything to do with me in any way.

At first, I was hurt that she would think so low of me to not even give me enough consideration to discuss the matter. After a while, I let it go. I realized it was her choice to cut me off, and I couldn't do anything about it. It was her loss, not mine. She made a judgment about me and pronounced me unworthy. How much of life we pass by because we judge instead of being open, forgiving, and taking the time to truly understand.

> You can't depend on your judgment when your imagination is out of focus.
>
> **Mark Twain**

Jesus said, "Judge not lest ye be judged," which I interpret to mean that if you are judgmental of others, you are really saying more about yourself. To condemn others, you are really condemning yourself. We have all made mistakes, so who are we to judge? Instead, we should use this as an opportunity to learn instead of branding people as unworthy.

Stop judging yourself or others. Stop trying to read their mind and determine what you think is their "motive" or "reason" for doing things. It's a burden to do so and will only serve to sow strife in your life, as well as in all those around you. You should always display respect while saying no to the behaviour.

Most of all, respect yourself. Instead condemning yourself for your mistakes, forgive, love, learn, and grow.

Radical Humility

Get Lost! Have you ever had someone say that to you? Well, I am here to tell you to **get lost**!

Now, before you leave the room in a huff, let me explain. When I say *get lost*, I am talking about developing an attitude of *Radical Humility*.

Do you have a big ego? Do you need to be first at everything? Do you think you're the cat's meow? To some degree we are like that in one way or another, but consider the following quote:

> *It is amazing what one can accomplish if one does not care who gets the credit.*

Funny thing is this quote is credited to two men: John Dove Isaacs and Harry S. Truman. Who actually said this quote? We don't know, and if we take the quote to heart, we don't care.

> When you are content to be simply yourself and don't compare or compete, everybody will respect you.
>
> **Lao-Tzu**

STRATEGIES FOR HAPPINESS

Stop for a moment and ponder what this quote is saying. Think of the impact it could have on the world if people would just take it to heart. "It is amazing what one can accomplish if one does not care who gets the credit."

> Class is an aura of confidence that is being sure without being cocky. Class has nothing to do with money. Class never runs scared. It is self-discipline and self-knowledge. It's the sure footedness that comes with having proved you can meet life.
>
> **Ann Landers**

Ray Schneider, an Assistant Professor in the Mathematics and Computer Science Department of Bridgewater College, Virginia, said "Let others clamor for the credit. Seek first the personal satisfaction of knowing that you have done well."

This is the essence of what it means to have Radical Humility. You are constantly doing your best knowing that it's something that is worthwhile and useful to the world, and then sitting back and enjoying the results. Whether you receive the credit is irrelevant. You know that you did a good job; you made a difference.

Jerry Weinberg, speaking to computer programmers in the book *The Psychology of Computer Programming* wrote:

> *Don't worry about the credit, even if your claims are just and true, You have done it and so now you can focus on improving your skills to do even more. Don't worry that the workplace may not be fair and objective in all cases.*

Radical Humility

I really enjoyed being a member of the Ottawa Welsh Choral Society. I hadn't been in a choir for a number of years and it was a real pleasure to be singing in a group again, hearing and feeling the harmony. One night at practice, I was singing away and the thought went through my mind, "Boy, am I doing well." I was enjoying the experience and how I was participating in it.

However, I didn't stop there. My brain continued in its narrative by saying "I'm doing better than anyone else." As soon as that thought finished crossing my brain, I was so ashamed. What did it matter if I was doing better or worse than anyone else? If I was doing the best I could and helping and contributing to the choir, then that was what was important. How could such a thing even be measured, and what would be the point? Having Radical Humility means you do your best and enjoy the doing, no matter what the result.

Someone who wrings their hands, mumbling how bad they are, and apologizing for their existence is not displaying Radical Humility, either. To do so is just as bad as someone who is conceited and always saying how important and wonderful he/she is. Both individuals are being self-absorbed and are actually saying "Look at me!"

To say "I am so wonderful" or "I am so pitiful" are both self-absorbed attitudes. People who are truly humble – truly egoless

---

Believe in yourself! Have faith in your abilities! Without a humble but reasonable confidence in your own powers you cannot be successful or happy.

Norman Vincent Peale

STRATEGIES FOR HAPPINESS

– can look at their life, assess themselves clearly, acknowledge where they do well, and enjoy it without fanfare. Or, they are able to identify where they need help and are neither afraid nor too arrogant to ask for it.

People who have Radical Humility treat themselves and others with respect. As the Bible says, "Do unto others as you would have them do unto you."

When you have Radical Humility, it does not mean that you allow people to walk all over you. It just means that being "number one" is irrelevant. You are balanced in your relationships. You care about yourself, but not at the expense of those around you.

It is important to be open to what others have to say. Someone may make comments that are hurtful, but if you confident in yourself, you can check to see if there is anything valid in the statement. If there is, then you can make the necessary changes. If not, then the Radically Humble person can just let it go. They are not threatened that others may not agree with them or believe the same way they do. They don't take things personally and out of context or waste any precious life energy fussing to trying to be right.

> He who is humble is confident and wise. He who brags is insecure and lacking.
>
> **Lisa Edmondson**

Taking things personally has always been a problem with me. I am learning to separate my sense of being from what others think of me. When facing situations that previously would have put me

Radical Humility

over the top, I am now better able to let them go, and even burst out laughing at the absurdity of it all.

With a healthy humility, you feel good about yourself. There is no need to prove anything. Self-respect is at the heart of true humility. Humility is being so secure in yourself, knowing your strengths and weaknesses, that you are at ease. There is no need for comparison in either a negative or positive way. When you have Radical Humility, you don't need to take the credit; you can just enjoy your contribution. It's a matter of being balanced in your views and relationships.

Now that you know that I am not trying to insult you, get lost! Loose yourself and become free.

Be Independent

One of my favorite shows as a child was *Tarzan*. There was one episode which always stuck in my mind in which Tarzan was on a raft with a number of other people, including children. They were trying to get to safety. In the blazing sun with little food and water, they had a long and dangerous trip ahead of them.

Tarzan instructed the adults that they were to feed themselves only and not the children, no matter how hard or cruel it seemed or how much the children cried. He wanted them to understand that even though the children would suffer, they would suffer even more if their parents gave them some of the food. They may feel better for eating, but if the parents did not have the strength to paddle to safety, they would all die.

Though this idea was not popular and against the instinct of the parents, it was in the best interests of everyone present. He didn't waste time worrying about what others thought of him or apologize for his actions. He did what he knew had to be done. Tarzan had to think independently of the good opinion of others in order to ensure his survival as well as the survival of those in his care.

BE INDEPENDENT

There are many ways we can learn to be independent. For example, when we stop worrying about what others think of us or stop comparing ourselves with others, either negatively or positively. When we bemoan the fact that others may be prettier than we are, have more money, or are more successful, we use up life's precious energy that we could be using to develop our own lives and enjoy what we have.

Self-worth that comes from a feeling of superiority over others is actually admission that we are less. If we need to pump ourselves up by putting others down, we are building on a phantom foundation. In reality, we are really giving away our personal power. Comparing ourselves in order to justify our existence, whether in a positive or negative way, will only lead to weakness.

> Man's ideal state is realized when he has fulfilled the purpose for which he is born. And what is it that reason demands of him? Something very easy – that he live in accordance with his own nature.
>
> **Lucius Annaeus Seneca**

True strength comes from knowing who you are, including all of your strengths and weaknesses, and being fine with it. It is also about working on the not-so-perfect parts when and where you can, while at the same time, without guilt or self-recrimination, accepting yourself totally, no matter what others may think. That is independence.

Our lives are a constant work in progress where we endeavour to become the best we can be. You don't have to have the material

Strategies for Happiness

possessions others have in order to be happy. All you need is to see the wonder you already possess. Everyone has something unique and beautiful to offer the world.

Society doesn't help us to be independent. We are constantly bombarded by the media and marketing through TV, articles, and ads telling us what we must look like, what we must own, and how to live to be happy. The problem is that many of those products are not there to make us any happier; they are there to make someone else richer. It's hard to live up to the standard they push. This is especially true for women, who continually compare themselves to all the gorgeous models.

The solution is to be the best you can, whatever that is at any given point in time. Be exactly who you are, not what you are told that others think you should be.

Being authentic and happy is the best beauty there is. We will never live up to the standard that society puts on us, nor do we need to. We should create our own standard of who we should be and what to look like, and live up to it. That is what it means to be authentic.

No matter what may be said, people who are physically attractive do have more of an advantage over others. To some degree, it makes sense that an attractive-looking specimen gives the impression, on some level, of being healthier, and therefore, more likely to produce children and carry on the race. In reality, it may be far from the truth, but it's human nature.

I didn't say it was fair – I just said it makes sense. After all, nature wants us to procreate. It does this by getting the two sexes

Be Independent

together for the mating dance. It is always throwing out bait through colour, sound, smell, and beauty. Nature doesn't care about worth; it just wants you to make babies.

Fortunately, we can choose to go beyond the limits that nature might put on us. There is so much more to who and what we are beyond what is physical. While beauty may be a plus to help one to succeed in some aspects of life, it does not guarantee happiness. That someone may not be so attractive is irrelevant. The ability to be independent of the way others think about us is not only freeing, but makes us very attractive.

So whether you are upset because you are not as good looking as others, or that you may have a false sense of pride because you perceive you are better than others, understand that you need to find your value just for being, instead of being better or worse than others.

> To be obliged to beg our daily happiness from others bespeaks a more lamentable poverty than that of him who begs his daily bread.
>
> **Charles Caleb Colton**

In order to achieve happiness, it is important to create your own standard to live by. Find out what makes you happiest and let that shine as your beauty – again, the ability to be independent of what others think, especially about you.

If you don't care what others think, how others look or act no longer matters either. If you are going to compare yourself to anyone, let it be you alone. You decide what needs to change and do

STRATEGIES FOR HAPPINESS

whatever it takes to make it happen. Develop yourself to be the best you can be, and leave others to do the same for themselves. Instead of complaining about what is not right about your life, take whatever action necessary to make it right, whatever that might mean to you. The things others have that you think would make your life so great may be nothing more than stuff.

It's important to be authentically you – to be the best you can be, inside and out. Look your best, act your best, feel your best, and don't spend time worrying about how you compare to others.

> It does not matter what others think, it is of prime importance, however, what you think about you. You can never do your best, which should always be your trademark, if you are cutting corners and shirking responsibilities. You are special. Act it.
>
> **Og Mandino**

There might be a temptation to change yourself in order to live up to external expectations. Trying to be what you think others want you to be will only frustrate and build anger and bitterness. It is only by being totally true to yourself that will you be able to be independent of others opinions and filled with genuine happiness.

Be yourself and not a clone of someone else. There is only one person who has the right or ability to give approval for your existence, and that is *you*. Don't relinquish that power to anyone else.

Life will often throw garbage your way. You never know when it's going to happen. You can't live your life in fear of those moments, nor can you be ready for them. If you develop yourself to be the best you can be, you will be better prepared to face those difficult times.

Be Independent

Be Authentic

Honesty is the best policy. Happiness cannot be achieved if we are deceitful or dishonest. Lying, cheating, and stealing will only bring about negative results. When you do these things to others, you not only hurt them, but damage yourself as well.

One of the biggest problems is that many people are not fully honest with themselves. They convince themselves that the way they act or the things they do are for their own good or for the good of those around them. They think that they have the right to be hurtful.

Self-deceit leads only to self-defeat. You have to be totally honest with yourself. You have to be able to face your faults and honestly look at who your are and what you need to do in order to make a positive difference in your life.

Are you living the life you want, or the life that others think you should be living? If your desires and goals align with those of other people in your life, great. However, if you are living a life dictated by others, and it does not ring true to your inner-most being, then you need to break free. Have the courage to stand up and say, "Hey world, this is me! I am fantastic just as I am. This is what I want to do and be." In other words, don't let others define you.

On the other side of the coin, happiness cannot come at the expense of others. There is a difference between what is best for you (positive self-interest) and thoughtless action to get your way (being self-absorbed). Though positive self-interest is an important aspect of happiness, if it crosses over and your actions are detrimental to others, then only misery will be the result all around.

Strategies for Happiness

It's in your best interest to be loving, thoughtful, and respectful of others even if the impulse is to think they don't deserve it. Your self-interest is not served when you degrade and destroy others, no matter how good it may feel at the time. Refraining from doing so demonstrates strength, courage, and integrity.

At the same time, be firm about your needs, goals, desires, and dreams. Positive self-interest is about taking care of yourself first, thereby enabling you to serve others. When you go on a plane, the flight attendants always go through the safety procedures. They make a point of saying that in the event of the cabins losing air pressure, the oxygen masks come down. They continue by saying in the case of small children, the adults should always put on their mask first, before they assist their children. After all, if the adults pass out, what good are they to the children? Tarzan would approve.

> I care not what others think of what I do, but I care very much about what I think of what I do! That is character!
>
> **Theodore Roosevelt**

How many of you work hard at taking care of your loved ones, but take no time to take care of yourself? What good will you do them if you are dead? Take the time to eat well, get enough rest, and develop your mind and body.

Positive self-interest is about being independent of what others think you should be doing, knowing your own worth, and taking whatever steps necessary towards becoming the happiest and healthiest you. A wonderful by product of this is that your joy will overflow to those around you. And *that* is a good thing.

Choose Courage

One day, I would like to own a cottage by the ocean. Sounds lovely, except for one thing. I realized that if I had a cottage, I would often be there by myself. This thought struck me with terror. It's not that I can't enjoy being by myself; in fact, I really do. The problem is at night, when it gets dark. My imagination starts to go wild.

The what-ifs start to flood my brain. What if I fell and hurt myself? What if there was a monster storm that swept me away? What if burglars broke in and beat me up? What if the cottage were haunted? (Okay, I realize it's unlikely that the cottage would be haunted, unlike the possibility of my being abducted by aliens!)

> Never let the fear of striking out get in your way.
>
> ***Babe Ruth***

Fear is at the root of all that causes us pain. Almost every negative experience can be traced to some sort of fear. Happy people use courage to combat fear. Courage is not the lack of fear, but the strength to face it.

Strategies for Happiness

Happiness is a choice. Fear immobilizes and freezes you from action. If you cannot take action because you are caught and held still by fear, the ability to make decisions is near to impossible, resulting in misery.

It is important to remember that fear is an emotion, based on what we believe will or could happen to us because of a particular circumstance. If we face the fear and see it for what it is, we can decide to overcome the fear. The first step is to make the decision that you want to change the way you think, the second is to challenge your beliefs about your fears, and the final step, taking the necessary actions to overcome it.

> This is the art of courage: to see things as they are and still believe that the victory lies not with those who avoid the bad, but those who taste, in living awareness, every drop of the good.
>
> **Victoria Lincoln**

What is a fear that has paralyzed you? Maybe it's the fear of rejection, failure, or even success. It may even be the thought that you may be found out as a fraud.

Some fears are well-founded, while others may seem to most people as far-fetched. However, it doesn't really matter where they come from or how silly they may seem because to you, they are real. Fear is very personal. What bothers one person may not be an issue to another. Whatever the fear, it is real in the power it may have over you. It can be something learned from our family, friends, or the society we grew up in. Many of our fears are ones we taught ourselves. We decide what we choose to fear.

CHOOSE COURAGE

Growing up, I wanted to be accepted and loved, but didn't feel worthy. I was afraid that people wouldn't or didn't like me. Maybe that was true for a number of them, but not all. However I made the assumption that people would just reject me. I accepted this idea as truth. I felt unworthy of attaining my dreams and goals, and was afraid that if I succeeded, I would be found out as a fraud and everyone would laugh at me.

I am so grateful that I am learning to name my fears and confront them. I remind myself daily to choose not to be held in their power. Empowerment comes from choosing to either overcome my fears or act in spite of them.

It's possible that the thing we fear may happen. There are no guarantees either way. However, when you compare what is possible with what is probable, you see your chances are slim that they will actually come to pass. While you can't turn a blind eye to danger, you don't need to be ruled by it either. Instead, head the possible off at the pass. Take action to ensure the best possible outcome.

> Happiness is a form of courage.
> **Holbrook Jackson**

I had a long list of reasons why I should not pursue my dream of owning a cottage. My fears ranged from the possible to the ridiculous, and I didn't even own the place yet. If I stopped just because of the what-ifs, then I was giving up before I even started. I realized that if I wanted that dream, I had to face my fear and nip it in the bud.

Strategies for Happiness

To overcome a fear that I might get hurt, I could find out about all the latest gadgets to help keep me safe, such as alarms and communication devices. I could take courses in self-defence and first aid. If I were worried about bad weather, I could make sure that my cottage was in a safe location, constructed properly, and had a well-equipped pantry and storm cellar.

> Courage is not the absence of fear, but rather the judgement that something else is more important than fear.
>
> **Ambrose Redmoon**

When dealing with fear, it might be wise to take baby-steps to prepare. Take it for a test drive. So I rented a cottage on Lake Erie for a week. This let me see how I might handle being on my own and work on overcoming my fears. It also gave me a chance to consider what I might want in my dream cottage, so I would know what to look for.

The first night by myself was a bit unnerving. I kept the lights on in my bedroom, and watched videos on my computer until I was dead tired. Every night, it got easier to go to bed. I was very sad to leave when my week was over, and I can't wait to go back again.

There may be nasty events in our future, but being afraid of them is not going to do a thing from stopping them from coming. When we are afraid that something bad is going to happen, and when we let it stop us from going forward with our life or enjoying the moment because of what might be, we are lost.

Does any of the energy that we put into our fear actually do anything to stop whatever we fear from happening? No! So instead, take

CHOOSE COURAGE

that energy, experience the moment, and decide to live to the fullest. Seize the day!

Ask yourself, what is the worst possible thing that could happen to you in any particular situation? Make sure to do this exercise either on a piece of paper or in your journal, not just in your head. The act of writing it down makes it more real.

Create three columns. In the first column, list your fears. Don't consider what others think of your fears or that they may judge them as being petty or silly. They are your fears, and you need to deal with them, so disregard what others think.

Next, assign each item a grade of possibility of happening: 0 being never going to happen, through to 5: no doubt it's going to happen.

In the second column, ask yourself why you think it scares you. Do not judge your answer; just write down everything that comes to your head. Brainstorm and let your thoughts flow. Again, do not judge the results.

> Courage is resistance to fear, mastery of fear – not absence of fear. Except a creature be part coward, it is not a compliment to say it is brave.
>
> **Mark Twain**

In the third column, brainstorm again and think up some ideas as to what possible actions you could take. Your actions could include researching information on what scares you, taking a course, or even just letting it go. However, you must take action. Just thinking about it will not be enough.

STRATEGIES FOR HAPPINESS

By writing down and putting a name to your fear, it often loses its power. You can't anticipate everything that is going to happen in your life, but by being pro-active, you will enhance your peace of mind. It's about stepping out of your comfort zone and trying new things instead of being frozen in indecision and doubt. It's not about eradicating your fear, but about taking action in spite of it.

This strategy will not ensure everything will be alright, but will give you positive ideas that will free you from the prison that fear can put you in. After all, the majority of what we fear never comes to pass anyway, so why sweat it until it actually happens? You can never be fully-prepared for what is to come, so do your best in the meantime.

Give yourself permission to free yourself from your fears and don't let them ever stop you from doing what you want to do.

Take Control

Handy gadgets, those TV remote controls. Why, I remember when I was young, we had to get up from our chair, walk over to the TV, and turn the dial. By hand! It's annoying when the darn thing doesn't work. You bang it a few times, only to realize that the batteries are dead. I just hate it when the batteries die. It makes me so mad. Now I have to get up off the couch. That's just awful. Stupid thing – it should work. Oh well, it's just a piece of junk, anyway! I feel a scream coming!

I guess I am overreacting just a bit. I should take a moment and calm down and think this through. Have you ever caught yourself getting really upset about something and then realizing that it was actually very insignificant? Don't you feel foolish?

For instance, you are watching TV with your significant other or your children. Someone other than you has the remote control. They push the buttons, passing by shows you want to watch and pausing too long on things that are of no interest to you. You want to rip the thing right out of their hand. They are pushing the buttons for you, and you don't like it. Ask yourself, who's in control of your remote? Who's pushing your buttons?

Strategies for Happiness

Think about all the people and events that push your buttons and send you over the top. Let's talk about why this happens, and some things that can overcome it.

> Parents know how to push your buttons because, hey, they sewed them on.
>
> **Camryn Manheim**

I suggest you take a look at the book called *How to Stop People from Pushing Your Buttons* by Dr. Albert Ellis and Arthur Lange. In this simple but insightful book, the authors acknowledge how hard life can sometimes seem to be. There is so much stress with companies going out of business, people losing their jobs, and families facing so many challenges. Our lives have become so fast-paced that we have to deal with many frustrations and hardships.

There are many opportunities to have our buttons pushed. This book gives excellent and practical ideas to help you cope and overcome the temptation to blow your stack when others irritate you.

According to the authors, there are only three things that humans can do: think, feel and behave. They continue by saying, "... if we're going to keep people and things from pushing our buttons, we'd better learn how to direct and control the way we respond mentally, emotionally, and behaviorally to button-pushers."

To help in coping with lifes' challenges, Ellis and Lange share the ABCs of button pushing. This is a three step process that we go through when our buttons are pushed. Being aware of these ABCs, we are in a better position to deal with these irritants.

TAKE CONTROL

The first step is A, or the *Activating Event*. Examples are individuals who irritate you or when your gadgets break down. Maybe you made specific plans you were really looking forward to, only to realize they have fallen apart.

Let's skip to Step 3, or C, which stands for *Consequence*. Something happens to irritate us. The end result may be that we overreact by becoming angry and lashing out. Maybe you have good reason to react the way you do, but does it feel good, and is it productive?

A is the *Activating Event*, what started it all, and C is the *Consequence* or end result. What about B, you might be asking? Yes, B. That is a very important step indeed.

Step B stands for *Beliefs* about the *Activating Event*. In the ABC process, B is a point in time where you are analyzing the situation and making a decision about how to react. It may just be a split second, but it's a definite point in time. In that split second, we make a choice as to how to react. Will it be positive or in anger and bitterness?

It can happen so fast, we often don't even recognize it is happening, and therefore believe that we have no choice in the matter. The reaction is to say that it is only natural to be upset. It just happened, and there was no time to think. However, the reality is that there is an actual point in time that our brain takes to register the event and make a decision about how to react.

Benjamin Libet is a neurosurgeon who discovered there is a lapse in time between when an individual decides to take action and when they actually do it. He called it the "life-change quarter-

STRATEGIES FOR HAPPINESS

second". This split second offers you the chance to stop yourself from taking negative action. You can use this time to change how you look at the event and therefore avert making it worse.

In that moment, you make a choice. You decide to get angry and overreact, or you decide to be in control of your emotions. It is a decision by which you can exercise the strength to make a constructive decision to let go of your frustration and anger.

Again, that doesn't mean that you let people run your life. Instead, it's a matter of pausing to consider what may happen if you overreact, get angry, and end up doing or saying something you might regret.

A cool head will not only help to resolve problems quicker and more productively, but also will help to make better decisions. If anger becomes your motivation, things may be said and done that will be regrettable.

So the next time you are faced with an unpleasant situation, remember that split second. Recognize it and make sure to use it to choose control. Smile and say, "Thank you for sharing," and then walk away. Or stop and listen to the pain the other person may be expressing. Be open to what you can learn. Act with intelligence and compassion, not blind reaction.

Realize what the possible consequences of your actions are. You are in charge of your personal Remote Control. Push the buttons wisely.

CREATE YOUR OWN MEANING

A friend once said to me, "There is no meaning to life, except what we create." At the time, I thought she was nuts. Now, I understand. How we view the world around us is indeed a matter of choice. We need to choose wisely.

It may not seem that way. We look at our beliefs and say, "I didn't choose that; that is the way I always thought about the world." However, at some point in our life, we were presented with an idea of what to believe about existence, and we either agreed to it or rejected it.

> What is the meaning of life? To be happy and useful.
> **The Dalai Lama**

On the other hand, we may be cognizant of making a choice about what to believe about our existence and place in the universe, including views about God or not, how we should live our life, etc. Whatever the decision, it feels so right and real. We may even see dramatic changes in our life. All of this may be taken as evidence that our beliefs are indeed reality.

Strategies for Happiness

Now, I am not here to say that your beliefs are either true or false. It's not up to me to tell you how you should or should not believe about your place and purpose. I can determine my beliefs only for myself, including what my purpose and meaning in life is. Whatever I believe may be totally different than yours, but it resonates with me, so for me, it's real. The same goes for you.

What does life mean to you? Some will say that it is to glorify God. Others will say to do good and make a difference. Still others account for their purpose in life as raising their children. All of these ideas may have validity, but it still comes down to one thing. What have you decided that you value in life? What you value will determine what is the meaning of your life and give your a purpose for living.

> A rock pile ceases to be a rock pile the moment a single man contemplates it, bearing within him the image of a cathedral.
>
> **Antoine De Saint-Exupery**

The beauty of this concept is that you have the power to choose. Purpose and meaning are not lofty ideals that only a few can comprehend. You have the power, the right, and the responsibility to identify your life purpose. No one else can do it for you, nor should you allow them to.

With choice, there is power. If you are sure of what your purpose is, and if there is no doubt as to why you exist, good for you. Go for it with gusto. Embrace it, enjoy it, fulfill it. If you are not clear about your purpose and the meaning of your life, create it. You have so much in yourself to explore.

CREATE YOUR OWN MEANING

Having a sense of purpose gives meaning to our lives. The Bible says, "Without vision, the people perish." Fulfilled people know their lives count – that they have made a contribution to the world. It could be a small thing, such as making people smile. It could be a grand thing, such as searching for a cure for cancer. Either way, they know they have made a difference.

Why am I here? What is my reason for being? If you don't have an answer to this question, you could feel lost and without purpose.

Today, we have so many things that make our life easier and less stressful. Yet many seem so stressed out. You see many children who are easily bored and restless. Often, people have to have something going on, something to do or somewhere to go. They always have to have music playing, the TV on or something to distract them.

Maybe this is so because often people are feeling empty, lost, and without purpose. They feel a need to fill up their lives with noise so they don't have to face the fact they have no purpose in life.

I challenge you to create you own purpose if that is how you feel. Identify what you truly value. Be true to yourself, and don't get caught up in the idea that it has to serve others. Once you find a purpose that resonates with you, it will ultimately benefit the world as well, but you have to start with what is important to you.

It may be through a cause that is close to your heart for which you take a stand. You might want to find an opportunity to volunteer in your community, such as working with the homeless, driving people to appointments, or sharing your expertise with others through training or public speaking.

STRATEGIES FOR HAPPINESS

More than likely, you will have more than one thing that is of value to you. Be open to the idea that the purpose and meaning you create will also be multi-faceted. For instance, I have a friend who values his family highly and gives a lot of his time, money, and energy to taking care of them. He does it not because he feels obligated to do so, but because he values his family and it brings him pleasure to help them out.

However, he has other things in his life that he values. For over 15 years, he has volunteered at a local hospital. Every week, he drives patients to and from the hospital for appointments. It's just a simple thing, but it fills him with joy to know that he is making a difference in the lives of others.

> A man who becomes conscious of the responsibility he bears toward a human being who affectionately waits for him, or to an unfinished work, will never be able to throw away his life. He knows the "why" for his existence, and will be able to bear almost any "how."
>
> **Victor Frankl**

You may value the ability to express yourself through music, art, or words. It could be the desire to travel, explore the world, and learn about all the cultures the globe contains. It may be a thirst for knowledge and understanding of what makes the world tick. The key is to make sure it is indeed something you value – something that is important to you. Don't limit yourself in any way, but be open to all possibilities.

It's a trap to identify a purpose primarily on what you think you *should* be doing. If you go with what you truly value, it will ultimately benefit the world. If you go only on duty, you may miss

CREATE YOUR OWN MEANING

the opportunities to truly express your particular talents and abilities. Follow your heart and it will not only serve you well, but serve others, as well.

When you have a sense of purpose, you become fully alive and have such a sense of fulfillment. In order to develop meaning in your life, you need to examine what your natural inclinations and talents are, develop the skill you have, or discover new skills. In order to do this, you need to try things – all sorts of things, in order to find out what makes you tick.

This discovery takes action. You can't find it if you allow yourself to just sit in front of the TV, play video games, or do other passive activities. Try all sorts of things: join clubs, discover hobbies, take courses, travel, talk to people to see what things concern them, read. The list is endless. Be creative and open your mind to all the possibilities.

Think big, but don't overwhelm yourself. You can't save the entire world, nor do you need to. Just focus on what you truly value. By doing so, you will make a difference, however small, and it will have a ripple effect that will benefit all.

In the book, *Five People You Meet in Heaven*, Mitch Albom tells the story of Eddie, a man who lived his life in pain. He worked in an amusement park, maintaining the rides. He was a widower with no friends, little money, and seemingly no value or purpose to his life. He thought his life was a waste, and that he had accomplished nothing.

He dies and goes to heaven, and through a series of revelations, finds out that because of his efforts keeping the rides in top working

STRATEGIES FOR HAPPINESS

condition, thousands of children were kept safe while enjoying the pleasures of the rides. Though he finally came to the realization that his life did have meaning after all, he didn't understand this while he was alive. It's a sad thought that so many people go through their lives without realizing their worth.

> Although a man may have no jurisdiction over the fact of his existence, he can hold supreme command over the meaning of existence for him.
>
> **Norman Cousins**

If you are still stuck, let me give you an idea. Make your purpose in life to be the *best you* you can be. Work diligently on developing yourself, learning, growing, and most of all, loving yourself. If that is your major purpose, and you do it without judgment in a healthy and balanced manner, you cannot help but become a happier person, and your joy is sure to spill onto others.

Being the *best you* you can be is in everyone's best interests. After all, if you cannot value yourself, how can you value others? The Bible says "Love your neighbour as yourself." Make it your purpose to learn to truly love yourself. The world will thank you.

So, take a look right now at what it is that you truly value in your life. I hope that you are at the top of the list.

Be Self-Centred

Be self-centred. You heard me! I am telling you, in order to be happy, you need to be self-centred. I realize this is not the standard dictionary usage of the word self-centred, so let me explain.

When I say be self-centred, I don't mean to be self-absorbed, thinking only of yourself, doing whatever you feel like with no regard for how it will affect others. Instead, it is about being centred, well-grounded, and balanced. It's about taking care of yourself first-mentally, physically and otherwise; then you will be in the best possible position to help others.

> You, yourself, as much as anybody in the entire universe, deserve your love and affection.
>
> **Buddha**

This includes doing whatever it takes to make yourself authentically happy. Find out what your source of happiness is and go for it. Remember that hurting or harming others does not bring true happiness.

Strategies for Happiness

The more you have true joy, the more you will have to share with others around you. Real happiness has the wonderful effect of generating joy and good will to others. It's a win-win situation.

Positive Self-Interest

Being self-centred means that you are centred as a person. You know yourself well and are focused as to who you are and what you are willing to do in your life. You are not easily manipulated. You know when to say no. You take on tasks because you want to, not because you are guilted into it.

Everything you do should be in the pursuit of your own happiness. Don't be ashamed of this. This drive can spur us on to great things if it's fueled by positive self-interest. You need to take care of yourself first before you can help others. You need to follow your dreams, not the dreams of others. Even Mother Teresa was motivated by positive self-interest. It was in her self-interest to help the poor because it filled her with joy.

> Happiness, then, is at once the best and noblest and pleasantest thing in the world...we always choose it for itself and never for the sake of something else.
>
> **Aristotle**

Self-centred people (in the positive sense of the term) are those who have dedicated their lives to pursuing authentic happiness, that deep abiding joy. They are sure of themselves, and are free from the burdens of guilt, shame, pain, anger, hatred, and self-pity.

BE SELF-CENTRED

This type of person has no need to get the attention and sympathy of others by being a victim or by lashing out negatively at those around them. Instead, being centred, balanced and fulfilled, they radiate joy, which is contagious.

Being free from negative emotions and actions results in more joy and clear headedness; it's just so much more fun. Who would you rather associate with – those who are sulky and feeling sorry for themselves, always plotting revenge, or those who are cheerful and optimistic, finding solutions to their problems?

Just because you are happy does not mean that you don't see the need to change things and just sit back and do nothing. It does mean that if we see a need for change, we have the right motivation to make the change. Be careful of the battles you choose to fight.

Anger is a poor motivator. The belief is that anger gives us the energy to do something about things that are upsetting. While it may spur us into action, it often makes us look like fools in the end. A common reaction to situations that make us angry and frustrated is to scream and say, "It's not fair!" which is acting in victim mode. Being a victim is always a position of being powerless.

Anger is a legitimate feeling and one that should not be ignored; however, it is still something that we choose to feel. Use anger as a tool to identify the areas that need to be changed, then let them go.

There is so much horror in the world, and we need to do as much as possible to make our planet a better place. This can be done by taking a stand on the issues that we value. We are much better-equipped to make those changes if we have the strength of

STRATEGIES FOR HAPPINESS

joy and optimism behind us. Productivity, power, and lasting change comes with a clear head and a happy heart.

Anger Opens You to Manipulation

Imagine this. You are presented with an issue that really angers you. You are so incensed with emotion that in the heat of the moment, you declare, "Yes! I am going to do something about it!" Then, when it's all over, you look back and see that the incident was really not as serious as you had initially believed.

The realization hits that the cause being championed is actually someone else's battle, and they used you as a pawn to further their personal agenda. Being so distracted by your anger, an opportunity was missed to make a real and important change. I can tell you from experience, it's not a pleasant feeling.

I once owned a house in a small community outside Ottawa where we co-owned the property that centered on our houses. One of the other owners brought to our attention that there might be a problem with the structure of the houses, which had all been built by the same contractor. There was much discussion as to what were the best options for possible legal action.

At first I was upset about the possible problems. I joined the discussion and was considering what would be the best action to take. Then I stopped, stepped back, and took a broader look at the situation.

I did some research of my own and came to the conclusion that the issues that had been presented where not real. In fact, taking legal action was only going to damage relationships with the town,

BE SELF-CENTRED

and in the long haul, put us at a disadvantage and possibly lowering the value of the houses. We were actually being manipulated into taking action because of someone else's agenda, which was more about personal revenge than actual problems.

I was glad I got out of it when I did, but it was a scary reminder of how others can manipulate for their own gain. When you are self-centred, in other words, centred and secure in yourself, there is less chance of others using you.

Don't Shoulder Other People's Burdens

Do whatever you can to help others in need. Giving of yourself is a great source of happiness, but be careful. It is easy to get so caught up in another persons' pain that we take it upon our own shoulders.

Someone is in trouble. A solution has to be found! The wheels start turning in the mind in an effort to find a way to fix the problem. By taking possession of the problem, there becomes a need to resolve it. It's now our responsibility. Then, when a possible solution is found and advice is dispatched, our efforts may be ignored or spurred. Our thanks for all the effort is that we are hurt and frustrated, and the problem hasn't gone away.

It is important to feel empathy for other people when they are suffering. Often, we do have useful advice and insight that can help the person get through the situation, and ideas for solutions that could be the answer. However, the problem starts when we feel that our solution is the only one.

It's not productive to attempt to take control over someone else's problem, even if it seems to us to be for their own good. They do not

STRATEGIES FOR HAPPINESS

need to *fixed*, but instead, they should be allowed to decide their own path to resolution. You can help, but you must not control. As much as it may hurt you to watch, they need to do their own thing and make the final decision, no matter what the result. How else will they learn? If they do fail, it's important to be there to provide support and care, not to say "I told you so."

> It is useless and futile to try to change other people. The only person I can change is myself.
>
> **William Curtiss**

As much as I appreciate all the wisdom, advice, and help people have given me over the years, in the end, I was the one to make my choices, for good or bad, to learn from them, and know that my friends supported me, no matter how crazy the idea was.

Teach Others to Treat You Well

Have you ever heard yourself saying, "She/he makes me so mad. She/he is so mean to me. I don't know why I put up with her/him"? On the surface, it looks like something external has caused grief. However, the reality is that no one can cause you pain unless you agree to it.

Having said that, there is no reason why you have to accept bad treatment. While showing respect for others, no matter how they treat you, there is no reason that you have to just accept it when they disrespect you. Instead of choosing self-pity and blame, you need to stand up for yourself with the expectation that they will treat you with respect and courtesy. That's being self-centred.

Be Self-Centred

When you are treated poorly, confront the person(s) involved, but do it in a spirit of love and acceptance. When we tear down those who hurt or anger us, it may makes us feel a bit better about ourselves momentarily, but that is a trap. We sink to their level when we lash out, ultimately hurting us in the end.

You can't control how others behave toward you, but if you don't let them know that their behaviour is unacceptable, then nothing will happen.

When this happens, don't take their behavior personally. Remember that it's their problem, not yours. Be in control of your life and your state of being, and don't let others dictate how you feel. Don't waste your precious life energy on their problems.

You don't need to defend your point of view. Being self-centred means you know who you are and what you believe in and stand for. All you need to do is let others know that you will not be treated like dirt. Be strong and assertive, but be loving and forgiving at the same time.

Often, bad behaviour continues not out of malice, but because people are not even aware that something upsets you. They can't read your mind. While it shows great strength and courage to forgive, overlooking inappropriate behaviour may result in it continuing. Making them aware gives them the opportunity to change, learn, and grow, as well.

Then there are those who treat you badly, know it, and take pleasure in it. Again, don't just sit and stew. You need to take action and confront them. If they refuse to change, which they have the full

Strategies for Happiness

right to do, you have to decide if it is worthwhile keeping a relationship with them or moving on.

No matter how much you might think you need someone in your life, no relationship is worth the destruction of your own well-being. You have to decide what you will or will not live with.

Whatever your situation, don't allow others to put you down. You are worthy of respect, always. Demand and expect it from others, as well.

Change Yourself and Let Others Be

How often have we heard about people who got married and were miserable. They knew that their spouse was a certain way, but they believed once they were married or had children, etc., their spouse would change. This is both arrogant and unwise – not to mention, it just doesn't work.

You cannot expect people to change just because you want them to do so. In fact, if you do, you will only open yourself to being hurt and upset. While we might ask others to change, it's another thing to expect or demand that they do so. It just doesn't work. We cannot change others just to please us, we can only change ourselves or our circumstances.

Effective change will only happen if the person in question decides for himself or herself that they want or feel a need to change. It will not happen if they are guilted, badgered, or disrespected. On the surface, they may appear to have changed, but once the opportunity arises, they will revert to their old ways of thinking and acting.

BE SELF-CENTRED

Instead, concentrate on changing yourself. Change your attitude about the other person. Is it really important that they feel the same way that you do about things? Is it really a deal breaker if they don't remember to put the cap on the toothpaste? Do you want to pin all your happiness on whether the other person is going to remember to put the dishes away in the same way you expect?

So treat yourself and all those around you with the upmost respect, and don't expect anything less from anyone else. Be focused on what is in your personal self-interest by being grounded, balanced, and taking care of your body and mind. That is what it means to be self-centred in a positive way.

> When I was a young man, I wanted to change the world. I found it was difficult to change the world, so I tried to change my nation. When I found I couldn't change the nation, I began to focus on my town. I couldn't change the town and as an older man, I tried to change my family.
>
> Now, as an old man, I realize the only thing I can change is myself, and suddenly I realize that if long ago I had changed myself, I could have made an impact on my family. My family and I could have made an impact on our town. Their impact could have changed the nation and I could indeed have changed the world.
>
> ***an Unknown Monk (c. 1100 AD)***

The Power of Choice

I was lying on the bed in the hotel room. Mentally, I was sucking my thumb and in a fetal position. What a horrible day! I had taken on the task of facilitating a course that was out of my league and it had not gone well. To make it worse, I had to do this course for the entire week, and was terrified.

All I could think about was how bad it had been. I couldn't sleep. I couldn't eat. I was a basket case. How was I going to get through the week ahead?

Later that week I was up early in the morning preparing for another session. I could feel the tension in my stomach mounting. I was not looking forward to another day doing this course.

I remember looking at myself in the mirror. I stared into my eyes and said to my reflection, "All right. I have had just about enough of this. Stop feeling sorry for yourself. You can do this, and you are going to do this." I even started to laugh at myself and did a little happy dance in front of the mirror. From somewhere deep inside me I pulled out the strength I needed. I made the choice to stop feeling sorry for myself, just concentrate on being the best I could be, and let the rest go.

The Power of Choice

That day, I did a terrific job. I knew that I had overcome my fear and self-doubt.

Is your life a choice or a chance? Is the quality of your life an accident or dumb luck? I maintain that our life has little to do with chance and more to do with the choices we make, whether we are aware of it or not.

We make choices every day of our lives. Many of them are conscious, such as deciding what to wear to work, what to eat for breakfast, etc. Then there are others that we are not so aware of that can shape our personality and the flavour of our lives.

> If you want to be happy, be.
>
> **Leo Tolstoy**

Once, when going to a party, a friend made a comment that was really upsetting, which put me into a foul mood. I knew I wasn't going to have a good time, and that made me even more angry. Then I realized that I had a choice. I could continue being angry and miserable all evening, or I could snap out of it. I decided to go for the latter, and as a result, I had a great time.

It's a common belief that events in our life shape our character and personality. As discussed earlier with the ABCs of button pushing, it's not the actual events, but how we choose to react that does the shaping. If tragedy strikes, we can decide to let it defeat us, or we can decide to gather strength and rise above the situation. It's not what is done to us that's important, but how we decide to react to it.

Strategies for Happiness

One of the most important choices you need to make is to decide who is in control of your life. You can define the moment, or let it define you.

Are you an angry person? Are you bitter? Are you happy? We become the people we choose to be. The reasons we have certain views of life are not primarily because of the personality we are born with or the events we experience, but more so because of the choices we make.

I don't want to trivialize the suffering we all may face from time to time. Let's face it, living can be hazardous to our health. However, when tragedy strikes, we can decide to face it, deal with it and learn from it, or just give up.

When Terry Fox found out that he had cancer, I'm sure he was tempted to feel sorry for himself and just give in to the idea that he was a victim. Instead, he rose above the event, decided to make a difference, and use his personal tragedy to help others. He did this by attempting to run across Canada in order to make people more aware of cancer as well as raise funds for research. Unfortunately, the cancer did eventually take his life, but he didn't let it take his heart.

Indecision Takes Away Your Power

Fear of possibly making a wrong decision often blocks us from making choices. However, it's better to make a poor choice than no choice at all. At least then you can learn from it and change direction. If you get stuck in fear mode and don't make any choices, you never have the opportunity to grow. Indecision is also a decision but one that

The Power of Choice

can cause much stress as well as a feeling of helplessness. Blaming fate or chance only contributes to this helplessness. When you realize that it's the choices we make, not just chance events, that direct and shape our lives, we come into real power and freedom. There is power in making decisions. It can be very liberating.

> This is my "depressed stance." When you're depressed, it makes a lot of difference how you stand. The worst thing you can do is straighten up and hold your head high because then you'll start to feel better. If you're going to get any joy out of being depressed, you've got to stand like this.
>
> **Charlie Brown**

When we are aware of how our choices shape our life, we can see just how much power and control we have. We can then define what our life is to be, instead of just letting things happen because every choice we make, whether to act or not act, has an end result.

We choose, not only the actions we take, but the way we look at things, our thoughts and ideas. Whatever choices we make, whether they be physical or mental, there are always consequences or results. Therefore, we must be willing to accept the results we receive because of our choices. If we don't like the results, we need to change our choices.

For instance, if you decide to stay in a relationship that is of a negative nature, that is your choice; you will have to live with the result. As badly as that person treats you, you cannot really blame them for their actions, because you choose to stay. Don't say you cannot leave, because there is always a way. If you want

STRATEGIES FOR HAPPINESS

to live the best life, you will make the choice to remove yourself from that situation.

Stop making excuses. If you want to change your life for the better, ensure the choices you make facilitate the necessary change.

We have so many options to choose from. The key is realizing we have options and the power to make the choice. The power and energy in every decision moves us from one place to another. The power of a decision can change the world.

Like many others, I have had to deal with the problem of debt. I seemed to accept the idea that I was in debt, and had no choice in the matter. Then, one day, while attending a seminar on a completely different topic, the speaker made reference to the importance of getting out of debt. It was an off-hand remark about debt, but it started me thinking.

> Man's power of choice enables him to think like an angel or a devil, a king or a slave. Whatever he chooses, mind will create and manifest.
>
> **Frederick Bailes**

I had two options. To continue on the way I was living or commit to getting out of debt. In that split second, I made the decision. I knew deep down that I was going to get out of debt. I just needed to find out how.

The power of that decision changed my life. Not only am I working towards getting out of debt, but my life is much richer

The Power of Choice

– not just because I have less debt, but more importantly because I have more control of my life. Choosing to make decisions instead of just accepting what is, translates to empowerment. It means I am in control of my life.

Choice is Power

What matters is what you believe. Change your beliefs and thoughts, and you change your life. You choose what to believe and what to think about. In *What Happy People Know*, Dr. Baker describes choice as ". . . the voice of the heart. It's honesty in action." When we exercise choice, we are taking action giving us power. Often the problem with choice is that people don't realize they have options. There are so many possibilities available, but often we don't see what they are because we are engulfed in fear.

In *You Can Choose To Be Happy: Rise Above Anxiety, Anger, and Depression*, Dr. Tom G. Stevens says,

> *We are each responsible for our own happiness. Responsibility follows control. Since each person has more control over his or her own happiness than anyone else's, then each person has the greatest responsibility for his or her own happiness. Why should someone else be more responsible for my happiness then I am – or vice-versa?*

A key to choosing happiness is to recognize the fact that you can indeed make the decision to choose happiness. The quality of our life is a result of choices we make. Sometimes, it's hard to make

STRATEGIES FOR HAPPINESS

the choice for happiness. We may be really tired and feel we don't have the strength. Sometimes, on some level, we are enjoying the bad mood and want people to feel sorry for us.

> Action may not always bring happiness, but there is no happiness without action.
>
> **Benjamin Disraeli**

One of the many misconceptions that can ensnare us is believing the way we think we are is set in stone and that nothing can be done about it. "This is the way I am. I have always been this way, and I can't change." I have heard this from many people who think they have no power over their own happiness. They have been that way for so long that they think were just born that way and cannot change.

It's not so much that we can't change our thinking pattern, but instead of that, on some level, we have made the decision that we don't want to change. Each one of us is totally responsible for our own happiness. The ability to change how we think, act, and feel is in all of us. We just need to believe and take action.

You Have Many Options

An Army volunteer sat down to his first meal in the mess. He surveyed his plate and asked the mess sergeant, "Don't I get any choice?", "Yes," was the reply. "You take it – or you leave it." Often people, like the volunteer, come to believe their options are very limited. Fortunately, the truth is that we actually have many

The Power of Choice

options at our disposal; we just need to become aware of them. The key is to think outside the box to find the options that will best work for you.

When it comes to choosing happiness, realize that it is a valid option, one that only you have the right and responsibility to make for yourself. It will not only make life more enjoyable, but will create an atmosphere of joy that you can share.

Therefore, choosing happiness is not act of selfishness but a necessary action in order to ensure that we develop our best selves. If we do the work necessary to develop happiness in our life, not only will our life improve, but it will overflow all around us. The ultimate end result will be to bring happiness to the rest of the world.

Focus on the Positive

Don't ignore the negative in your life. The reality is there are many nasty things that will come our way, and we need to face and deal with them head on. While being aware of the negative aspects of our lives, it is important to shift your attention to things that empower you.

> Happiness is a conscious choice, not an automatic response.
> **Mildred Barthel**

When unfortunate things happen, resolve to find meaning that resonates with you. In his book *You Can Choose To Be Happy: Rise Above Anxiety, Anger, and Depression,* Dr. Stevens tells a story

STRATEGIES FOR HAPPINESS

about when he was a young boy. He was out for a drive with his father and brother. His father wanted to stop and speak to a friend and said he would be only a few minutes. Thirty minutes later, they were still in the car waiting for their father. They were getting angrier by the minute.

Then he realized that he was only hurting himself, so he decided to change his attitude. He did this by changing the focus of his anger towards his father to looking around at all the beauty that surrounded him. When his father did finally return, he was in a good mood because he decided to shift his attention to something positive.

> The history of free men is never really written by chance but by choice – their choice.
>
> **Dwight D. Eisenhower**

While your source of frustration may be much more intense and serious, remember that you always have choice as to how you will respond to it. Victor Frankl was a man who lived one of the worst experiences you could imagine.

In WWII, he was sent to a Nazi concentration camp. He suffered hunger, starvation, and pain. While many other prisoners gave up hope and died, he decided to live. He created his own positive imaginary world. Here, he looked for and found immense beauty, even in something as repulsive as a discarded fish head. With imagination, he had long conversations with his wife who had already been killed. After the war, he wrote a book called *Man's Search for Meaning* where he said

The Power of Choice

The salvation of man is through love and in love. I understood how a man who has nothing left in this world still may know bliss, be it only for a brief moment, in the contemplation of his beloved.

He wasn't happy about the war, but he found happiness within himself in order to survive. If Victor Frankl could find happiness within the horror of war, can't we do the same?

Use Pleasure Wisely

When I talk about making happiness our primary goal, don't get it confused with pleasure. Pleasure may make you feel good for a while, but it doesn't last. It is not necessarily a bad thing, but it's often temporary. When you develop your Happiness Potential, a common side effect is pleasure. Enjoy the pleasure, but don't live for it. Happiness is something much more deep and rewarding.

Pleasure can be obtained by hurting others, which of course, is only going to come back to hurt you in the end. This, of course, will not bring authentic happiness. Some people may find pleasure in taking revenge on others who have wronged them. There is no denying that, for some, this may be a pleasurable thing. However, it will not create a *happy being*.

Dr. Stevens says,

> *Maximizing happiness is different from maximizing pleasure. Pleasure is produced by lower brain centers responsible for getting our lower needs met. Pleasure does not care about other people's needs . . . Happiness is the*

Strategies for Happiness

only human state that measures our overall physical and mental well-being... It results from harmony among our inner parts. We cannot deny important parts of ourselves and be fully happy. We cannot neglect the future and be fully happy. Nor can we neglect others and be fully happy. Happiness and love go hand-in-hand. Loving someone means we value his or her happiness. When we feel love, we feel happy – whether the love is for an object, an activity, or a person.

Be Realistic and Honest

You will not be happy every moment of your life. When you are ill or experience tragedy, of course you will feel pain or "dis-ease". Some days you will do better than others. On the days you don't feel so good, don't give up. It does not mean you are a failure if sometimes you don't feel the happiness. Don't beat yourself up because of this. You can't force it, but you can make the choice to work toward it.

> Most folks are about as happy as they make up their minds to be.
> **Abraham Lincoln**

Allow yourself to be honest with your emotions. Have a good cry and let the emotion flow through you instead of trying to block it. Once you get it out of your system, pick yourself up and continue the journey. Whatever you do, don't get stuck in self-pity. At one point, you may need to force yourself to snap out of it.

The Power of Choice

Like I mentioned earlier, I looked in the mirror and said, "This is it, I have had enough of feeling bad. I am snapping out of it, right here, right now." I pointed to myself, smiled, and told myself to get over it and get going. Doing a happy dance, twirling around the room, I began to laugh at how ridiculous I looked.

Did this solve all my problems? No, but it sure helped to put me in a better frame of mind to deal with them. I made the choice to snap out of my negative state, instead of being held captive by it.

Remember to find the lesson in the moment, learn, and move on. As Dr. Stevens says:

> *The persons who become the happiest and grow the most are those who also make truth and their own personal growth primary values...You can fail to reach a goal, but you can never fail to learn.*

You always have options to choose from and it is your responsibility to find the best ones to suit your needs. There is no one way to accomplish it. It is as individual as each person that ever existed. Choosing happiness means finding the tools that are going to help you achieve happiness.

As we grow up, we are taught what to believe and how to behave in order to be a good person, a success, acceptable or lovable. When we believe in an idea, we have, in reality, agreed to it. On some level, we have said "Yes" to that idea. It becomes our reality.

Just because we say yes, does not mean that it's true or even healthy for us. Many of these ideas and concepts have validity and should be considered, but we need to examine what we agree to and

STRATEGIES FOR HAPPINESS

figure out what is truly valid and what is not. We need to agree that we have choices and then find the ones that will lead to happiness. We just need to agree to the idea that we have the power to make the necessary choices that will lead to happiness. It is all up to us.

The Happiness Habit

Make choosing happiness a habit. Take a look at how the website Dictionary.com defines a habit:

a. A recurrent, often unconscious pattern of behavior that is acquired through frequent repetition.

b. An established disposition of the mind or character.

In other words, it's something we do without thinking. We develop a habit by "frequent repetition". Happiness is not the feeling or buzz that comes with a pleasant event. It's a mindset – a way of thinking. Since we have total control over the way we think, then we have control of our emotions. We can develop a positive, happy mindset by cultivating happy habits.

You can develop your *happiness habit* by choosing to use happiness strategies outlined in this book, such as gratitude, forgiveness and claiming your personal power to name a few.

Why is it critical to develop the habit of happiness? Remember when London's subway was hit by terrorists? Fifty-one people died and many others suffered greatly. It's at times like this that it is so important to possess the habit of happiness. I was encouraged in reading that the day of the attack, people were still going about their business, socializing, and making it clear that in spite of the cruel

The Power of Choice

actions of others, they were determined to show that it was "business as usual". They were not going to let the bombing stop them from living. To do so would be to admit the terrorists had won.

> I am still determined to be cheerful and happy, in whatever situation I may be; for I have also learned from experience that the greater part of our happiness or misery depends upon our dispositions, and not upon our circumstances.
>
> ***Martha Washington***

I don't make light of the gravity of what happened, nor do I say we should just brush it under the rug and pretend it didn't happen. Those that did it should be brought to justice. What I do say is that it is imperative that, despite the horror, despite the cruel and incomprehensible motives and actions of these individuals, we need to make the choice to continue living our lives to the fullest and not give in to fear. Developing the habit of happiness means that we show full appreciation for what we have.

With gratitude and forgiveness, we have the power to not let these acts control us through anger and hatred, and to continue to find clarity of purpose and live that purpose every day. If we are able to do this, we will be the victors.

If happiness is not a habit with you, I challenge you to make the choice to start today by incorporating these ideas into your life. They say it takes at least 30 days to develop a new habit. Start now, and commit to expressing appreciation, extending forgiveness, ceasing the complaining and pursuing your dream.

Body Balance

My daughter Heather received free tickets to an old-fashioned carnival show that came to Ottawa. It was a 1930s-style circus that incorporated a freak show, a classic ferris wheel, and acrobats under a big top complete with sawdust, candy apples and wide-eyed kids.

The acrobatic show included a fantastic display of aerial trapeze, hoops, contortionism, juggling, and aerial tight rope and group shivaree. My, how they moved their bodies, with such grace, poise, and balance.

It made me think about how important balance is in all aspects of life. When we are in balance, mentally as well as physically, we are in the best position to fully enjoy ourselves. It doesn't take very much to throw off the balance, so it's important to do whatever it takes to make sure we maintain it.

As much as I believe that happiness is our choice, there are times when our bodies make it difficult to make that choice.

Sometimes, I am not feeling my usual positive self and I can't figure out why. I'm using the happiness strategies, and yet, I still feel bad. I have come to realize that sometimes there

BODY BALANCE

is something going on at a physical level and therefore needs a physical approach.

The body is a storehouse of chemicals. When the body is out of alignment and not performing to the best of its ability, your chemical balance gets out of whack and you feel the results. This may lead to feeling depressed and out of sorts.

A chemical imbalance is a physical thing, though it can be exacerbated by improper thinking. Beliefs have the ability to change our balance for better or worse.

There was a short period when I was seeing a psychiatrist for depression. I always knew that even though I was struggling, eventually I would come out of it, but it was a scary time. Fortunately, I have never sunk so deep that I would have considered suicide, though I understand why some people might want to. If I ever found myself feeling that way day after day, month after month, with no hope I would ever get out of it, it would be easy to see why people would want to end the pain.

> If depression is creeping up and must be faced, learn something about the nature of the beast: You may escape without a mauling.
>
> **Dr. R. W. Shepherd**

When pain is so intense, it's hard to think straight, making it difficult to really work through the problem. A chemical imbalance is something you might not be able to just talk yourself out of. Things are so heavy and so hard to deal with, that it's difficult to make the proper choices that lead to happiness. Our

STRATEGIES FOR HAPPINESS

bodies are tired of fighting and trying to do the right thing. It can be exhausting to work towards that which is best for us and so much easier to just give in, be angry and feel sorry for ourselves. There are times we just need some help to pull ourselves out of the pit.

There are so many experts in our life, and all of them are eager to tell us how to live. Sometimes, their advice is just what we need to hear, while other times, it may not be in our best interest. Some of these individuals may have experience and knowledge, or they may only think they do. While some experts should be respected as they are often learned people with much to share with the world, others we may need to take with a grain of salt.

There is a certain celebrity who thinks he has the truth. He proclaims there is no such thing as a chemical imbalance, that drugs have no part in our life and that psychiatry is wrong. He considers himself an expert, so we should do as he says. I don't think so.

In the end, we still have to take responsibility and find out what works for us – which treatment we are willing to participate in. It's a good idea to listen to what the experts have to say, though we are still the ones that need to make the final decision. When we learn to stand on our own two feet and determine the direction of our lives, there is less chance we will be swept away by the words of some so-called experts.

When the balance is out, how can it be corrected? The best way is through proper diet and exercise and doing what you can to produce the best possible mental attitude. The experts may suggest treatments such as surgery, therapy, or even drugs. Remember, that no matter what the choices or options the experts give you, the final decision is still up to you.

One of the first things my doctor suggested was an antidepressant. I refused. I didn't like the idea of using one. Some would say that I should have gone along with him and just done what he told me. After all, he was the expert. However, I decided that for me, the side effects were too risky.

This was my decision to not use drug therapy, and I believe it was the right one for me. However, I would never tell someone they should not do so. Though I am not a big fan of antidepressants, who am I to tell others what to do? Antidepressants may be just what they need to overcome their situation.

If this is something you are considering, you need to research and find out if the benefits of taking such drugs outweigh the possible problems. If you are so depressed you cannot think straight, maybe it's worth it to experience some of side effects, just until you get back on your feet.

> In order to change we must be sick and tired of being sick and tired.
> **Author Unknown**

I think that many people misunderstand what antidepressants do. They are not happy pills. They do not make you feel good. You don't get a high from them, like a narcotic. What they do is make you feel normal. They balance your state of mind, so that

Strategies for Happiness

you can then think straight. Then you have the ability to work on your problems.

When you are in the depths of depression, you can't think straight, and it's hard to see any hope. You are so full of pain, feeling helpless, or useless, that you don't want to even try. Everything seems so hopeless, so what is the point?

These drugs may help you to get your emotions leveled out, so you are then able to function normally. Though they may help, they are only a tool for clearing your head enabling you make the choices and decisions to get out of the situation that is causing you pain.

> If you have health, you probably will be happy, and if you have health and happiness, you have all the wealth you need, even if it is not all you want.
>
> **Elbert Hubbard**

The real cure is to get your body healthy and your mind balanced to make those choices. If nothing seems to work, and you are worn out from your depression, then maybe antidepressants may help. If you make the decision to give this kind of prescription a try, you do not need to feel ashamed.

However, before you go that route, you may want to consider some natural alternatives. One such alternative is a supplement called SAMe. It's a natural antidepressant that helped me through one of my darkest times. It's natural, healthy, works fast, and has few or no side effects. SAMe is short for S-adenosyl-L-methionine.

Body Balance

This is a chemical that is found naturally in our body. We experience problems if the levels are low. It plays an important part in the chemical processes of your body.

SAMe is involved in methyl-donor conversion, which means it is used in all sorts of chemical processes in your body. Sometimes, either because of age, stress or other factors, the levels of SAMe in the body become low, affecting your health and sense of well-being.

Another supplement that I've found very useful is called L-Theanine, an extract of Green Tea. It works by changing your brain wave pattern, which induces relaxation and calm. Again, it is not a happy pill, but just helps you to be clear, focused and calm. It is non-addictive and has no side effects.

I am not a doctor, so I am not telling you to use either prescription drugs or natural supplements. It's up to you to research, ask questions of the experts, examine the pros and cons, and find what works best for you, as well as doing whatever it takes to ensure your body is in optimal health.

Someone who is a wonderful example of this mindset is my friend Vicky. When I think of Vicky, I think of laughter. Everything seemed to make her smile and bubble with laughter. Whenever we get together, we are constantly laughing. She is one of those rare individuals that are such a pleasure to be with and have as a friend.

I first met her in high school. As a teenager, and going into my adult years – okay, most of my life – I have been somewhat fashion challenged.

Strategies for Happiness

She is always there, helping me improve my wardrobe, giving me knowledgeable advice about my hair, and teaching me how to do makeup. At least, trying to. Did I mention I am fashion challenged?

She always accepted me for just who I am. While others laughed at me, she laughed with me. Boy, did we laugh.

Then I noticed a change. She seemed to laugh less and to be struggling. It was hard to watch and would make me feel helpless as there was little I could do but try in my own small way to share my love and concern.

> Joy and happiness are the indicators of balance in a human machine... An inner joyousness, amounting to ecstasy, is the normal condition of the genius mind. Any lack of that joyousness develops body-destroying toxins. That inner ecstasy of the mind is the secret fountain of perpetual youth and strength in any man. He who finds it finds omnipotence and omniscience.
>
> **Walter Russell**

One thing I admire about Vicky, aside from her amazing smile and strength of character, is that she does not take anything lying down, wallowing in self-pity. In spite of her struggles, she made the decision that she was going to take action, whatever it might take, in order to resolve her problems.

She researched to educate herself and see what options she had to deal with the situation. Feeling that her doctor was not really servicing her in a way that was in her best interest, she found a new one. Prepared with her new found knowledge, she partnered with her new doctor to start to find solutions. She also

BODY BALANCE

sought out other alternative health options that would further enhance her mental and physical health. The next time I saw her, I noticed the difference. She was brighter, more vibrant, and much more like her old self. It is so good to be laughing again.

She is an example that you never have to just accept your situation, you can and should take whatever actions necessary to make your life the best it can be.

The experts are important and have many valuable tools and advice to give us such as eating right, exercising and drinking plenty of water. No matter what they say, in the end, you are still the one who is in control of your life. Don't shun the advice of the experts, but always make up your own mind as to what is good for you.

Embrace Failure

I was applying for a summer job in an office. When asked how fast I could type, I figured about 50 wpm. I was then asked to do a typing test. When this was done, I found out that not only did I not type 50 wpm, but I had more mistakes per minute than I had words. Needless to say, I didn't get the job. For a long time, I didn't go near a typewriter, if I could help it. I was a failure as a typist.

Then came the answer to this problem: the computer. I decided to take a course in word processing. Because there were only two computers in the room and about 20 students, we had to take turns. We were told to work on typewriters until it was our turn to actually touch the magical machines.

Again, my typing skill was displayed in full glory. My teacher made it clear that I would never make it as a typist, even with the wondrous computers. She indicated that though they were very forgiving, you still had to type fast. Had I given in to the temptation to give up, failure would have won the day.

So, instead, I bought my own computer. I taught myself the popular word processing package-of-the-day and went to town. I figured I could make lots of money typing other people's papers.

Embrace Failure

My first contract was for a university student that was desperate to get a paper in on time. It did not go well. I ended up not charging that poor student for my efforts, seeing as I probably caused him to fail the course.

Still, I didn't give up and continued to work on my skills. I proved my teacher had been wrong as I eventually did learn how to type well and fast, thanks to my trusty PC. Mind you, I would not ever consider using a typewriter.

There is a school of thought that says that you should never, ever, ever give up – that true failure is not when you don't succeed at something, but if you stop trying. In the Disney movie *The Haunted Mansion*, the main character was trying to get back into the mansion to save his wife and children. He tried many things, but just couldn't get in. He sat there in dismay and self-defeat.

He was asked what he was doing and replied that he tried and tried, but couldn't get in and was a failure. It was pointed out to him that he had tried and failed numerous times but that he only really failed when he stop trying.

This is sound advise, as long as each time you try, you examine your actions, and figure out why it didn't work. Then change you action plan and try again. Make sure you don't do the exact same thing continually and expect different results as that is a sign of insanity.

True failure is when you either let the unrealized goal ruin you or when the pain of the lack of success controls you. It's when you look at the unsuccessful event and say, "See, this is proof that I am a failure," instead of saying, "Well, I tried and found

STRATEGIES FOR HAPPINESS

it wasn't for me." Even worse, true failure is being so afraid of failure that you don't even try.

Sometimes, you have to give up on a dream. There can be freedom in letting go. I am not saying give up because the thing is too hard. You often have to work hard to achieve your dreams. There can come a point where you are using way too much personal energy for little gain, when there could be other things you could be doing that would be even better. You may be focusing so much on "not giving up" that you miss the boat on other opportunities that could work even better.

> A man may fall many times but he won't be a failure until he says someone pushed him.
>
> **Elmer G. Letterman**

The trick is recognizing the difference. Making mistakes or not achieving the goals you set out to do is not failure, just a learning experience.

Changing the direction of your focus, adjusting your goals to fit your new knowledge and maybe even changing you goals completely are perfectly acceptable as long as you are learning, adapting, and not giving up on yourself. If there comes a time that you decide that continuing is not in your best interest – that the goal no longer serves you, don't consider yourself a failure. The ultimate failure is to never even try because of fear. Some people are so afraid of failure that they never even try. They will never know the exhilaration of the dream. They are stuck in their mediocre world, safe in their harbour of the mundane.

Embrace Failure

Maybe you failed to attain your goal, but at least you tried. You have had the chance to spread your wings and gain an experience. This shows courage, curiosity, and creativity.

You don't have to go through you life wondering *what if*. You now can put your energies into finding out *what's next*. Celebrate your failures, learn from them, share what you have learned and continue in the search for your passion.

Failure Can be Blessing in Disguise

At some point, you may have to stop and examine what you are doing. Maybe you are approaching something in the wrong way and this venture is not for you. You need to look at other options. There are many different ways to getting the results you want.

If you do come to the conclusion that the goal you desire is not in your best interest, take the opportunity to glean any lessons you can from the experience and move on. Take what you have learned, change your direction, and find something else that, though different, is just as wonderful.

In may turn out that whatever it was you were trying to achieve was not what you really wanted or needed. Trying things out gives you the opportunity to experience things and see how things fits in your life. If you seemingly fail at something, it could be because you are using the wrong approach, or it just isn't what you need. Never look at the failure as a negative thing, but as a chance to learn and grow.

Do your best, but when it doesn't go well, don't beat yourself up over it. Instead, forgive yourself. Feel free to make mistakes,

STRATEGIES FOR HAPPINESS

as they often teach us our greatest lessons. Like the lesson of how not to do something. Our experience helps us to understand that we either really do not want something, or that there is a better way of doing it.

Change is Good

When you experience failure, it gives you an opportunity to take stock of your life. What things are good? What things are not so good? What do you need to change? What things are fine the way they are?

If there is something in your life that needs changing, then gather the courage to make the change. It doesn't matter how far you have gone; it's not too late to change. It's better to cut your losses and make the necessary change to start new and fresh than to just hold on to an old behaviour, person, place or thing that causes so much pain.

Don't be afraid of change because you think that this is the way you have always done it or that it was the way you were taught to do it. Maybe you have invested so much time and energy that it would be a waste to give it up now. If it does not bring you joy and fulfillment, if it doesn't help you to fulfill your purpose, then maybe you need to let it go.

If a relationship brings you only pain and sadness, is it worth keeping? If that second car is only a status symbol and the frustration of keeping up the payments is overbearing, is it worth it?

I once allowed myself to sign up for a club that promised me I would save so much money. I had to pay a large fee up front and then a very small fee for the next ten years, and in exchange I would be able to use their services in order to purchase products at a very

Embrace Failure

reduced rate. After signing up, I soon found that it did not live up to its promise. I kicked myself for having been talked into this, but in the end, it had been my choice.

After making the down payment on this service, I was faced with having to pay the yearly fee. I tried to figure out whether it was worth the cost. What about all the money I had invested in it? If I quit, it would all be lost. Should I go on, or just quit and cut my losses?

I finally decided to drop this albatross. It didn't solve all my financial woes, but it freed up some cash that would put me on that road to being debt-free. It was painful to admit that I had made such a foolish decision, that I had wasted so much money and that I might be losing out on a big chance to save a lot of money. In the end, I did it. Another lesson learned. I don't regret letting it go.

Failure is not a bad thing. In fact, the only real failure is if you give up before you attain a positive result even if it turns out to be very different from your original vision. Not trying at all is even worse because you will never know what could have been. Instead of being afraid of failure, be afraid to accomplishing nothing, which is the worst of all fates.

It's kind of fun to do the impossible.

Walter Elias Disney

Learn the Lesson of Pain

Children can be such a joy and such a pain in the neck. Don't misunderstand me, I love my children dearly, and I am grateful every day for them, yet, over the years, they constantly tried my patience. At the same time, they taught me many valuable lessons.

I remember when they were very young. Though I had so much to be grateful for, I was not a happy person. I was in an empty, loveless marriage. I was always struggling with money, or the lack of it. It seemed to me that I had a lot of problems and sometimes had a hard time trying to move forward.

At least, that was my perception.

One day I was at a flea market with my sisters. I came across some cute little purses that I thought I might buy for my girls. They were furry pouches, with long thin straps. I imagined what their reactions would be when I presented the gifts, how their eyes would light up with joy and appreciation.

I had a problem, though. Money. I didn't have much and was constantly worried about it. I felt guilty if I spent too much, especially on such frivolous things.

LEARN THE LESSON OF PAIN

I went to my sisters and showed them the purses. I expressed how I wanted to get then for my girls, but I wasn't sure if I should buy them. After all, money was short.

I did not expect the reaction I got from my sisters. I was expecting loving support and understanding. What I got was anger and disgust. Apparently, money was all I ever talked about. They were tired of my constant whining.

I was stunned and stung. I felt attacked, violated, and totally misunderstood. How dare they say such things about me? I didn't whine about money all the time.

After all, my situation was tough. I had it bad. They should have had more sympathy for me. I was the person who was struggling to make it through life. I was the person in a bad marriage. I was the person with two small children, etc. etc. etc.

To top it off, when I did finally decide to buy the purses and gave them to my daughters, they were not interested in the least. After all that, they didn't even like them.

> If you're going through hell, keep going
> **Sir Winston Churchill**

For years I carried the pain of that incident – the ouch of the stigma I supposedly carried. I was angry that my sisters treated me so and that they didn't even try to understand.

Now, I could have continued to wallow in my pain and misery, feeling sorry for myself and blaming everyone else. Instead, I came to a point where I decided to uncover a lesson in the pain.

STRATEGIES FOR HAPPINESS

Here is what I learned. I am the person in charge of and responsible for my life and well-being. My happiness comes not from waiting for others to validate me and make me feel good about myself, but by realizing that I can choose my attitude and response to whatever happens. Life presents us with many experiences in order to learn. Some are painful.

> Painful as it may be, a significant emotional event can be the catalyst for choosing a direction that serves us – and those around us – more effectively. Look for the learning.
>
> **Eric Allenbaugh**

Looking back, I think I did have a reason for being hurt. My sisters could maybe have been more sensitive to my need in that vulnerable moment. They were somewhat harsh. At the same time, I also realize they were right. I was too focused on me, myself and I. I was trying to get external validation – pity – to be the heroine inside my little soap opera, my drama of victimization.

Now I am more aware when I start to fall into this trap. I recognize I am doing it and I step back and say, "No! I will not allow myself to get sucked up in it again! My happiness is much more important then that. I no longer want to be that sad creature."

Next time you feel a mental ouch, stop and listen to what is going on inside of you heart and head. Don't judge; just listen. Ask what is the possible lesson you need to learn from the experience.

It may sound something like this, "Hey everyone, look at me, look at me. Please pity poor me. You should pity me because I have it so bad. Please tell me that you feel sorry for me. That way I can

Learn the Lesson of Pain

tell you know I am here, you feel sorry for me and I can become the centre of your universe. Tell me I am a poor creature and that I am such a tragic hero because of all I endure."

I know what you are thinking. You are saying, "I don't talk like that," but let me assure you that if you are hurt, bitter, or afraid, you do. If you are really honest with yourself, you will hear some version of this speech, and, I speak from experience, it will not give you the result you expect or desire. It will only make others frustrated with you. I know; I've been there.

If your voice is telling you that you should feel sorry for yourself, that others have wronged you and that people should pity you, stop! Refuse to listen to such rubbish. You are the creator of the quality of your life. You and only you! No one else can touch you, unless you agree to the pain. Say no and let it go.

Find the lesson your pain has to teach you. What attitudes do you need to change? How about habits you may need to modify? Do you need to give or seek forgiveness? Do you need to become more physically active or eat better quality food? Can you be more assertive in your relationships, or maybe more respectful?

Once you have learned your particular lesson, take whatever action necessary, and with a heart full of gratitude, embrace all the wonders in your life.

> If you will call your troubles experiences, and remember that every experience develops some latent force within you, you will grow vigorous and happy, however adverse your circumstances may seem to be.
>
> **John Heywood**

Purge the Pity Party

I was driving to work in a funk. The closer I got to the office, the more I was grumbling under my breath. I drove into the parking lot, my frustration and disdain building minute by minute. I didn't want to go to work. I didn't enjoy my job and I was frustrated that I couldn't do the things I wanted to do.

As I was getting out of my car, the most amazing thing happened to me. I heard a voice speak to me. It said, "Are you feeling sorry for yourself?"

That question made me laugh and all of a sudden, the gloom was gone. Vanished. Out of there. I didn't even have to analyze what I was feeling sorry about. I just knew that I had been, and the realization lifted me out of it.

When I realized that I had allowed myself to wallow in self-pity, I immediately snapped out of it. When I became acutely aware of what was happening, I acknowledged it and was then was able to do something about it. It's like AA; the first step is to acknowledge you have a problem.

I have heard about people hearing voices, but had never had it happen to me. Actually, to say it was a voice, like someone was

PURGE THE PITY PARTY

standing next to me speaking into my ear, doesn't really describe it. It was more like a thought, a very strong and distinct thought, that crashed into my head – a thought that came, but not from my thinking.

Anyway, whatever you might think about my sanity at that moment, it was an amazing experience. I stopped in my tracks and listened. Yes, I was feeling sorry for myself. I was resentful that I had to get out of my comfy bed that morning and get ready to go to a job that I hated. I was frustrated that I had to endure a day of tedium, instead of pursuing what I really wanted to do. I was angry about a whole bunch of other little, seemingly unimportant and petty things the world was throwing my way.

When I started to acknowledge all the wonderful things I had in my life to be grateful for and how far I had come in working towards my goals, my attitude and mood changed dramatically.

> Self-pity is our worst enemy and if we yield to it, we can never do anything wise in this world.
>
> **Helen Keller**

Becoming aware of my foul state of mind allowed me to make the choice to act differently. The effect was immediate and wonderful. I was no longer glum and resentful. I was full of joy and appreciation for the job at hand.

Even though my job was not what I really wanted to do, it was a stepping stone towards my passion. It paid my bills and taught me many skills that would be useful as I progressed towards my goals.

Strategies for Happiness

As I continued to walk to my office, I realized that although my mood had changed, there was still some residual negativity. Then I heard the voice come again. This time it asked me, "What are you afraid of?" What? Afraid? I wasn't aware I was afraid of anything in particular.

> Self-pity gets you nowhere. One must have the adventurous daring to accept oneself as a bundle of possibilities and undertake the most interesting game in the world making the most of one's best.
>
> **Harry Emerson Fosdick**

Having learned an important lesson from the voice before, I started to examine myself and realized that I indeed had some fears that were affecting my mind and heart.

Failure had been such a big issue with me over the years. I had tried so many things and it seemed, at least in my mind, that most of the time I failed. I had so many thoughts race through my head, judging and condemning me for all my mistakes. These thoughts were critical, while the voice I had just heard was gentle and loving.

Have you ever stopped to listen to your thoughts and hear what they have to say about you? It's not always pretty. Often we say all sorts of horrible things to ourselves. T. Harv Eker, author of *Secrets of the Millionaire Mind* would call this mind-frick.

It's important to be aware of what your mind-frick is saying so you are able to dispute it. Whatever you do, don't agree with it; don't let it have control. My mind-frick was trying to tell me I had failed so many times, and this would be no different and was trying to convince me I had a big F for failure tattooed on my forehead.

Purge the Pity Party

To make matters worse, I also realized I was equally afraid of succeeding, and not being deserving of it. If I succeeded, I would have a new set of responsibilities to live up to, which would be a lot of hard work. With awareness, I was able to identify and then deal with the thoughts. I came to realized that I was actually very successful. Not only was I not a failure, but I had handled success quite well.

Face the Emotion Honestly

Happiness is a state of being, not a state of feeling. We can be happy beings who, from time to time, experience negative emotions. When this happens it is not a good idea to just sweep them under the rug and expect them to go away. Sometimes, you need to allow yourself to feel the negative emotion in order to purge it from your system.

> Self-pity is easily the most destructive of the nonpharmaceutical narcotics; it is addictive, gives momentary pleasure and separates the victim from reality.
>
> **John W. Gardner**

Negative thoughts and emotions should not be ignored. Instead, light needs to be shed on their existence in order to effectively eliminate them. You don't need to understand all the reasons they are there; you just need make the choice to have a healthy and constructive response to them. Give yourself permission to take a moment, feel the pain, have a good cry, maybe scream a little bit, and get it out of your system. Once you have done that, let it go. Don't dwell on it or wallow in the situation.

STRATEGIES FOR HAPPINESS

I am grateful for this experience because it taught me to examine my frame of mind anytime I am in a bad mood. Now when it happens, I ask myself the same questions. I actively look for those things that I have allowed myself to feel sorry about – no matter what the significance – check my fears, and focus on gratitude.

Your mind can't handle being both in a pitying and a grateful state. I would rather be grateful and full of appreciation than full of the misery of self-pity. I once saw a sign which read, "If you are not happy and grateful to be alive everyday, your ego is running your life." In this context, ego is another way of describing victim mentality.

I am not saying that in order to overcome self-pity, you need to hear voices in your head. When you are feeling down, just ask yourself those two simple questions: "Am I feeling sorry for myself?" and "What am I afraid of?" Being aware is key to being happy.

I don't need the voice to remind me, though I would be open to hearing it again. Something tells me that little voice is very wise.

Happiness is not a reward – it is a consequence. Suffering is not a punishment – it is a result.

Robert Green Ingersoll

The Jigsaw Puzzle

My daughter Rebecca used to love jigsaw puzzles. She would take up the whole living room when working on them and for days we would have to tippy-toe carefully around so as not to disturb them. Then, when it was finished, she would just take the puzzle, break it up, and put it back in the box.

Picture yourself working on a very complicated puzzle, one of those 500 - 1000 piece jobs. Piece by piece the picture forms as you feverishly anticipate the result.

You might look for all the outside pieces and make a frame, then fill it up, watching the picture take shape and form. Referring to the picture on the box, you watch the progress.

Finally, you come to that climactic moment. You are about to feel the joy and sense of accomplishment as you plunk down that last piece. You can just feel the click of that piece going into place.

Your hand moves to pick up that final piece but it's not there! You feel around, certain that you just saw it. You look all around the table, under the chair, in the box, but nothing – it's just not there. It doesn't matter that most of the picture is there, splendid in its colour

Strategies for Happiness

and glory. No, one piece is missing, and that's all that matters. What a disappointment! All that work for nothing. Ouch!

That's often how we view our life. Unless everything is perfect, unless all the pieces are present and fit according to plan, we are not happy. That is not realistic. If perfection is what we are waiting for in order to be happy, we never will be.

> Seize from every moment its unique novelty, and do not prepare your joys.
>
> **André Gide**

We may have all sorts of wonderful things in our life, except that one piece is missing – one little aspect of our life that's not perfect. There's one small item that's not there, and that's all we can think about.

Are you living your life like a jigsaw with a missing piece? It may be such a beautiful work of art, everything fits well and looks great, but we focus on what is missing, and miss out on all that we do have. That one little piece can be a source of pain, frustration and depression stemming from a lack of appreciation of what we do have.

What is your missing piece? It will vary from person to person and depends on what you value most. I don't dismiss the reality that the missing piece is important to you. I'm sure the pain is real. However, I encourage you to stop focusing on what is missing and celebrate all that you have. Otherwise, you will drive yourself insane.

THE JIGSAW PUZZLE

There are many reasons why the missing piece may cause so much pain. Let's examine three of them; focus, image and expectation.

Focus

First, let's take a look at focus. If we focus on the one piece that is missing from our puzzle, all we can see is that little blank space. You don't look at the rest of the puzzle – the amazing picture that is your life. You don't see all the hard work and effort you put into it, how far you have come, or what you have achieved. All you can see is that you are a failure. You might call yourself stupid for having lost that piece. Like Homer Simpson you might hit your head and yelp, "d'oh!"

> Keep in mind, your moods are primarily the result of what you focus on.
>
> **Mike Brescia**

Instead, you must stop obsessing over that blank space. Pull your eyes away from that piece and celebrate all the beautiful tapestry of your life. Look at your life as a whole and realize all that you have accomplished and contributed. Nobody is a failure unless all they can see is that one little hole.

Image

It's upsetting when a piece is missing from the puzzle, making the picture imperfect. We grow up with a picture in our head of what our ideal life should be. When the ideal doesn't come true, or

STRATEGIES FOR HAPPINESS

the perfect picture is somehow shattered by reality, we may allow ourselves to become bitter because life does not work out the way we want it to.

When I was young, I had an image of what I wanted for my life. I looked forward to getting married, having children, and being loved and adored. When I did get married, it didn't unfold the way I had envisioned it and eventually it ended.

One day, I was walking down the street and I saw a young family just ahead of me. There was a man and a woman walking with their children. They seemed so happy and loving, enjoying each other and their children. I was filled with such sadness and longing. I didn't have that, and it looked like I was never going to have it. My marriage was a failure. I was a failure. My dream had died.

> When one door of happiness closes, another opens; but often we look so long at the closed door that we do not see the one which has been opened for us.
>
> ***Helen Keller***

Fortunately, I didn't allow myself to dwell on these thoughts for long. I quickly realized that even if my dreams hadn't worked out exactly as I had hoped, I was far from a failure. I only needed to stop focusing on the blank spaces. I re-evaluated my dreams and found new ones.

I further realized that even though my marriage didn't live up to my dream, I could appreciate it as a valuable and worthwhile experience. Our relationship had its problems, but we had many a

The Jigsaw Puzzle

good time as well. I am grateful for having shared my life with him, even if it didn't last.

It helped to make me who I am today. I learned to be stronger, the importance of not holding a grudge and the power of giving and asking for forgiveness. I recognized that I need to take responsibility for my part in my marriage's breakdown.

Since then, I have found other things to fill my life – new and exciting adventures. All these lessons made me better able to stand on my own two feet and enjoy just being me. So, when the time came that I did meet someone to share my life with, the new relationship was on a better foundation.

The best thing about my first marriage is that I have two of the most wonderful children anyone could ever want. They are my most treasured jigsaw pieces.

It is not wrong to have an ideal to work toward – an image of what our dreams look like, but be flexible with the image. Allow the image to change with the circumstance as you learn more about yourself and your potential.

Expectation

This brings us to the third reason why the missing pieces may make us unhappy. Expectations! As we are working away at the jigsaw, we're anticipating the end. It is important to be realistic and make sure that our expectations are not beyond the realm of possibility.

We are expecting the pleasure we will feel when we complete the work. Often we build up our expectation way too high, so that

STRATEGIES FOR HAPPINESS

when the event finally happens, it may fall far short of what we had hoped for and dreamed of.

Before I went to Panama with my mother, we planned the trip for a year. It was promising to be an exceptional time. As we got closer to the day we would be leaving, people started to say to me, "You must be getting so excited! I bet you can hardly wait. It's going to be so good!"

Well, I was definitely looking forward to it, but I was trying not to put any kind of expectation on it. I wanted it to be whatever it was going to be. If I tried too hard to anticipate all that was going to happen, I might set myself up for disappointment. Also, when your expectations are too rigid, you might lose out on the joy of the unexpected. As it turned out, I did have a wonderful time because I was free to enjoy a very special time with my mother.

> The world we have created is a product of our thinking; it cannot be changed without changing our thinking.
>
> **Albert Einstein**

Expectations also frustrate us when the thing we are expecting doesn't even happen. Just imagine, you plan something for months and the day arrives when bang, it all falls apart. This is going to happen, it's part of life – but we must not let it destroy our life.

While it's a good idea to plan and look forward to things in the future, just remember that we must not allow our expectations to have too much power over us. Learn to enjoy where you are at this very moment.

THE JIGSAW PUZZLE

Expectations can be fun, but it can become a source of unhappiness if you fall into the temptation of feeling entitled. When people feel that they are entitled to something, they lose their appreciation for that thing and everything they already have. The result is none other than unhappiness.

This sense of entitlement can destroy the most essential element of happiness in anyone's life: Gratitude! If you feel the world owes you, and you are entitled to something, when it does come your way, you will not truly appreciate it. You will feel cheated and misused. If you don't get what you feel is owed to you, you will become bitter and angry. The more gratitude you develop in your life, the happier you will be – guaranteed.

Expectations are good things when you focus on the possibility without being tied down to the end result. They can give you a positive goal to look towards, as long as we don't get out of sorts when things don't happen exactly as planned. Therefore, expect that you will have a good life. Expect that people will treat you well. Expect that your children will behave properly. And if these things do not come to pass as expected, let it go.

Dealing with the Blank Space

So how do you deal with the missing pieces in your life? How do you live with that little blank space on the Jigsaw that is your life? What you need to do is take stock of the magnificent picture that is your life and develop a proper appreciation of it. Then you need to look at that missing piece and make a decision. Either find something to fill up that space, or decide to learn to live without it.

STRATEGIES FOR HAPPINESS

First of all, acknowledge that there is a piece missing. To the best of your ability, identify what it is. Second, ask yourself how important this missing piece is to your health and happiness. Is it something you truly want? Third, either find a way to obtain the missing piece, just forget about it, or find a suitable alternative.

If you really feel the need to have this item, do whatever it takes to get it, while being realistic. Question yourself intensely to be sure it's an essential part of your being. If you can't convince yourself, totally, that the item is indispensable, you need to either forget about it or find something else that may be just as good. In the end, you might find that you were either better off without it, or that whatever alternative you came up with was even better.

> Live all you can; it's a mistake not to. It doesn't so much matter what you do in particular, so long as you have your life. If you haven't had that, what have you had?
>
> **Henry James**

What are some items that people often consider their little blank space to be? One of the biggest missing pieces that can cause so much pain is what they may perceive as a lack of love – romantic love to be specific. The desire for a relationship is one of the driving forces in our life. After all, nature wants us to find a mate and propagate the species. Aside from that, it's just a very enjoyable experience.

However, it's something you can't force. You can't make another person love you. If you wait around for that special someone to sweep you off your feet and make all your problems go away, you could be missing out on many exciting and truly fulfilling experiences. Don't

The Jigsaw Puzzle

say to yourself, "Poor me, I am stuck here at home with no one special to do anything with." Instead of concentrating on that piece, concentrate on developing yourself to be the *best you* you can be, by learning to love yourself unconditionally.

You already have a relationship with the most wonderful person in the world – *you*! Give yourself permission to love yourself and do whatever it takes to develop your talents, skills and abilities and share them with the world. Concentrate on loving yourself first, fully, unashamedly, with passion and joy. If you don't love yourself, it will be harder for others to love you, as well. This is the best way to prepare for that special someone, and if they never show up, you are still a winner.

When I became single again, it was suggested that I change from my married name to my maiden name, Hedley. There was nothing wrong with my married name. My children proudly bear it, and so they should. However, I considered what it might be like to take my father's name back. Yet, the idea of being Donna Hedley filled me with loathing. Poor, sad, unlovable Donna. When I thought about her, all I saw was a lonely, funny-looking, fat, ugly, stupid little girl that everyone made fun of. I didn't want that again. She had many blank spaces in her life.

After learning many of the lessons I share in this book, I began to fill in those blank spaces with a new perception of who and what Donna Hedley was. I realized that she was actually a bright, happy, exciting, beautiful, talented, and very lovable person. She was a worthwhile human being, not because of anything she did, but just because she was. I decided what was the jigsaw of my life. So I am a Hedley again, and loving it.

STRATEGIES FOR HAPPINESS

Though I still wanted to have someone special in my life, I decided I didn't need him in order to be happy. The first New Year's on my own was looking to be somewhat lonely. The girls had gone to spend the evening with their father, and I had not been invited to any party or get-together. I sat there wondering what I should do, just go to bed, watch TV or feel sorry for myself. Then I decided that no, I wasn't going to sit around. Just because I had no one to spend the evening with did not mean I could not enjoy myself.

I jumped into my car, drove to Ottawa, and went out to dinner in one of my favorite restaurants. Next, I went to see a movie, and finally, I went to Parliament Hill to watch the fireworks. All-in-all, I really enjoyed myself. That was the first of many such adventures. Instead of focusing on what was lacking in my life – my blank space – I focused on living it to the fullest, celebrating who and what I was at that moment in time.

Eventually I did find someone special, but when we got together, it was because we chose to be together and because we enjoyed each other's company, not because we felt we had to have a relationship to be of value. If I had never met him, I could still have been a happy, healthy person because I learned to love myself.

This was one of my little blank spaces or missing jigsaw puzzle piece. Yours might be completely different. Whatever it is, decide what you are going to do with it. Is it something you simply must have? Is it something that you can really live without? Is there some alternative that could give you the same satisfaction?

Celebrate the wonder of who you are, including all your warts and wrinkles. Find your missing piece and fill it with the love, joy and gratitude that only you can provide.

Eradicate Envy

I wanted to become a desktop publisher, or, as Kathleen would say, an "electronic pre-press designer." I was working as an administrative assistant, which is a fancy word for secretary, and had played around with some desktop publishing (DTP) software, in the hope of changing careers. I created some simple documents but nothing that was taken seriously.

There was another person in the organization I was working for who also wanted to become a DTPer. One day she was given the opportunity to work on a layout project that would develop and showcase her ability. She was so excited and happy. I, on the other hand, was very jealous. I wanted to do that job.

> You can't be envious and happy at the same time.
> **Frank Tyger**

I was tempted to be angry at her good fortune and wallow in self-pity. Why should she get the opportunity, and not I? I could have allowed myself to stew, but instead, I decided to wish her well. Either my opportunity would come someday, or I would find something better to do.

Strategies for Happiness

Being envious was not going to help me achieve my goal any faster. As it turned out, I continued to work toward my goal of becoming a DTPer. I developed my skills, learned more about the business, and created a portfolio of my work.

One day, out of the blue, I received a phone call from someone who had interviewed me for a job the previous year. I didn't get that job, but he remembered my work. A position had just opened up to manage all their publications, and he was offering it to me. This was a wonderful opportunity – much better than the one I had been envious of.

Don't Allow Envy into Your Life

Envy is an ugly thing and does nothing to enhance your happiness potential or your dreams. Instead, it fills you with a sense of failure and entitlement. It's an indication that you don't think very highly of yourself. Wishing harm on others that have what you want is not only a statement about your character but an indicator of the possibility of your success in life. Jennifer James, an urban cultural anthropologist and faculty member of the Psychiatry and Behavioral Sciences Department at the University of Washington said:

> *Jealousy is simply and clearly the fear that you do not have value. Jealousy scans for evidence to prove the point – that others will be preferred and rewarded more than you. There is only one alternative – self-value. If you cannot love yourself, you will not believe that you are loved. You will always think it's a mistake or luck. Take your eyes off others and turn the scanner within.*

ERADICATE ENVY

Find the seeds of your jealousy, clear the old voices and experiences. Put all the energy into building your personal and emotional security. Then you will be the one others envy, and you can remember the pain and reach out to them.

When faced with such a situation, make the decision to join with others in their joy. Rejoice with them in their good fortune. Congratulate them and wish them well. Do what you can to help them with their goals and talents.

What will you get out of this? Well, for one thing, you will be happy. You will not be controlled by envy and malice toward others. Just because they have achieved what you want does not mean you cannot, someday, achieve it yourself. Also, if you are in the right frame of mind and open to the opportunity, they may be there to help you to get to where you want to be. The key is to have the strength and wisdom to be grateful, even if it's not you that has achieved the goal. Your time will come.

> Envy is an insult to oneself.
>
> **Yevgeny Yevtushenko**

The more we help and promote each other in our endeavors, the more we build up ourselves. Getting angry at someone because they were successful will only end up hurting us.

That doesn't mean allowing others to take advantage of us but in spite of their treatment we need to be conscious, loving and helpful whatever way we can. Not for what we can get out of it, but because

Strategies for Happiness

the more we build each other up and make the world a saner, healthier, happier place, the better it is for all of us. If we promote each other and help each other along, we will be in a better position to achieve the best kind of life.

Are You the Best One for the Job?

There were times I have been disappointed from not getting something I felt I really wanted and deserved. However, upon reflection, I realized that I may not have been the best person for the job, and had I been the successful candidate it, I would not have enjoyed it.

> The envious man thinks that if his neighbor breaks a leg, he will be able to walk better himself.
>
> **Helmut Schoeck**

In high school, I was always involved in music. I loved being in the choir. I took it seriously and tried to be the best choir member I could be. I was even picked to be in a smaller group that accompanied the choir. Yes, I was the cream of the crop.

One year, the teachers went on a work-to-rule campaign. This meant they would work during school hours, but would not do anything extra. There was an evening event coming up where both the choir and band would be performing. A decision had to be made as to whether it should be canceled as there could be no teachers present to supervise.

The decision was made to pick someone from the choir who could take over as choir conductor for the evening. I wanted so

ERADICATE ENVY

much to be the chosen one. When the decision was made, they picked . . . someone else. Yep, they didn't pick me. The evening came, we all got up to perform, and then it happened! The student director that had been picked did a marvelous job. Yep, they sure had chosen the right person.

The end of the school year came, the work-to-rule was over, and the teachers were back at their posts. We had a final evening performance and awards ceremony. Every year they had a music award for whomever did the best and the most for the choir. I figured I had worked hard for the choir all these years. I had put a lot of blood, sweat and tears into it. I gave it my all. Finally, I was going to win, and all my efforts would be recognized.

The moment arrived, and I was waiting anxiously to go and claim my prize. The presenter got up and said "And the award for excellence for the choir is . . ." not me. No, it was my friend that had been the student choir director. Hey, I was supposed to win this time.

I was crushed, but knew, deep down inside, that she really had deserved the award. She had done a terrific job in leading the choir through the crisis. When I was honest with myself, I realized I did not yet have the skills needed to do the job. So, I rejoiced in her good fortune, and released my envy. I would have saved myself a lot of pain and misery if I had not allowed envy to cloud my judgment and poison my outlook.

Envy is really about agreeing with the concept of being unworthy. When caught in envy's trap, the pain of what you think you are missing can be so intense it can blind you from seeing all the wonders you already have.

Strategies for Happiness

As the American journalist Harold Coffin said, "Envy is the art of counting the other fellow's blessings instead of your own." We need to rise above our childish demands and expectations. While anticipating future rewards for our hard work, celebrate when others are succeeding as well.

> Envy is a symptom of lack of appreciation of our own uniqueness and self worth. Each of us has something to give that no one else has.
>
> **Unknown**

Just because someone gets there before us doesn't mean we are any less worthy or that we will never attain it eventually. We just have to keep on working toward our goal. When we celebrate others' victories, we can learn from them and consequently helping us to get there eventually.

Overcome envy by wishing others well. Next time you feel the green monster rising, look at the person you are jealous of, and silently – or maybe not so silently – bless them in their good fortune with sincerity and appreciation. Encourage them to continue to succeed. Your time will come, and then they can celebrate with you.

CREATE YOUR OPPORTUNITIES

My friend had a dream to become a sailor. He wanted to buy a boat, learn how to sail, and live on the ocean. He took courses, bought the boat, learned and practiced what he needed in order to realize his dream.

Though his goal did not materialize exactly as planned and he ended up selling his boat and settling in Ottawa, he did not regret all the time, effort, and money he had invested. He enjoyed every minute, learned new skills, and was quite happy to be settled on land. In addition, he occasionally goes on sailing trips, all the better prepared for them. It had not been a waste of time. He had, in fact, become a sailor, even if it was part-time.

He could have given up by saying, "I'm too old . . . I don't have the money . . . I don't know what to do." Instead, he knew what he wanted, and created the atmosphere in which it could happen.

There is so much to do, learn, and experience in life that there's never a reason to ever get bored. Take the initiative and create your own opportunities. No matter what happens, when you are proactive, you are in the driver's seat of your life.

STRATEGIES FOR HAPPINESS

What do you want from life? If you are not sure, don't just sit around waiting for something to just happen to you because you may not like the results. You can create your own opportunities by finding a need and filling it.

Develop new interests, start a hobby, take courses, volunteer. This may sound simplistic, but it's really worthwhile. Write a book. Whether you publish it or not doesn't matter. The exercise of researching and writing will help you to develop new skills and ideas. If you do publish it, bonus!

Give your new interests an honest try. It may take a few attempts to come to appreciate it. If you give up on the first try because you didn't like it, you might be missing an opportunity.

> You must learn day by day, year by year to broaden your horizon. The more things you love, the more you are interested in, the more you enjoy, the more you are indignant about, the more you have left when anything happens.
>
> **Ethel Barrymore**

Take Responsibility

Being pro-active means you are taking responsibility for your life. Though your parents, spouse, and friends all want you to be as happy as possible, they can't do it for you. Only you have the power and the right to do that for your life. Your happiness is in your hands! Make the choice to focus on your happiness, and then take the actions to achieve it. You are in control.

Things do happen to us that are not our fault. It's so easy to just say, "It's out of my hands. . . I can't do anything about it. . .

CREATE YOUR OPPORTUNITES

it's all his/her fault." However, it would be better to cultivate the ability to respond to our situation, rather then just reacting. When we take responsibility for everything that goes on in our life, we are in power. Being accountable for our reaction to events is an important step towards greater happiness.

Taking responsibility will create an abundance of freedom in your life. If you take responsibility, who can hurt you, who can get the best of you, who can abuse you? Your attitude and decisions are in your control. To understand this is to understand just how powerful you are, which is so liberating.

Creating opportunities is all about finding a way to see your dreams come true on your terms. It is not measuring success by what the world says, but by what you say.

If you want to be a singer, don't measure success by the idea that you are discovered, have an album, and adoring fans. Being rich and famous may be nice, but if singing is what you crave, then sing.

It doesn't matter to whom. It can be in your basement. Maybe jamming with friends or by getting a gig at a local bar. This may not be as glamorous as being a famous rock star, but you are singing, and that is what is really important. Sing for your own enjoyment and don't worry about what others think. It is such a shame that people will not allow themselves the joy of singing just because other people think their voice is bad.

I once worked on a project that had gone into maintenance mode. There was little new work, and I was getting frustrated and bored. Then the lesson of responsibility hit me again. I was in control

STRATEGIES FOR HAPPINESS

of my life and therefore had choices. No one but me was forcing me to stay in that situation.

I decided to take action. I started to look for other projects. I seriously looked at my options in self-employment and started taking action towards that goal. I used my time to do whatever it took to make my life better.

> No one's happiness but my own is in my power to achieve or to destroy.
>
> **Ayn Rand**

Not only did this push me toward a more rewarding career, but it re-enforced the importance of not complaining, not pointing fingers, and not feeling sorry for myself, but instead, taking control.

Since I stopped blaming my boss for my situation, I freed myself from the anger and resentment that I was beginning to accumulate. Not only did this give me positive energy that I used to create my own life to be the way I wanted, but it kept me from souring my relationship with my co-workers. Who knows when you are going to need those relationships in the future?

I am grateful I learned to be pro-active, that I can take charge of my actions and attitudes. I can and must take responsibility for my life, and by doing so, take control of my life. This concept transformed my way of thinking and living. So start today – take charge and make opportunities happen in your life.

Focus on What You Want

My sister Kathleen always said I was too honest for my own good. I thought she was kidding but I now believe there is some truth to it. Though I hate lying and deceit, it's not to say I have never done either. I have to admit, I have, and am ashamed when I have succumbed to them. However, being too honest has its issues.

The problem with my being too honest is that I look at the good and bad in everything. When I have an experience, I analyze it (and often over-analyze it). I may say "That was fun and I enjoyed it because of this or that." However, I don't stop there. The honest part of me kicks in and I start to vocalize what I didn't like. So, for a period of time I focus on what I don't want or like.

> The key to success is to focus our conscious mind on things we desire – not things we fear.
>
> **Brian Tracy**

Honesty is a good thing, right? It most certainly is! So, when I talk about what I don't like, I am being totally honest about the

Strategies for Happiness

situation. Or maybe I am using honesty as a means to justify the opportunity to complain.

Oh, how we love to complain. It's such a pleasure to find others who understand our pain and enjoy putting in their two cents' worth. While it may feel good to hear others join you on your rant, complaining may cause more problems by once again making you focus on what you don't want in your life.

In the book, *Secrets of the Millionaire Mind*, T. Harv Eker says that complaining makes us a *crap magnet*. In other words, the more we complain, the more we attract negative events into our lives. He puts forth a challenge to go a whole week without any complaining, and how it has transformed lives.

There is a lot of talk about thinking positively and focusing on what you want and not what you don't want. Some people say that what you focus on expands, so if you focus on what is bad, you will get more of it. If you focus on what you want, you will get more of that. When I am stating, however innocently, about what I don't like about a situation, then I am going to get more of it.

How do I overcome this urge to share the negatives of my experience and still be true to my honesty and integrity? You can't ignore the nasty in your life or in the world around you, but you can take part in the solution. Though having positive thoughts may not solve all your problems, they can help to shape your beliefs. If you have strong, healthy beliefs about yourself and the world around you, your thoughts will reflect that. If you have a positive mindset and outlook, you are in a better frame of mind and creativity to find solutions to the problems.

Focus on What You Want

Once I went for training to develop my skills as an IT instructor. We had to do mini-demos of our teaching style and technique. Afterwards, we were evaluated, and feedback was given to help us improve our performance.

We were told that in giving feedback, we were to never start with what they did wrong or what we didn't like about the presentation. Instead, we were told that we had to start off by sharing with the individual what we liked best about what they did.

After we shared as much encouragement as we could, we then were to proceed to the areas to improve. It was to be stated in a positive manner. We were to say "Next time, how about trying this . . ." We would give the person an idea of how to take something we thought they could improve on and do it better.

So instead of saying "You should not look at your notes so much," we would say, "Next time try looking at the audience more and maintain good eye contact with them."

> The successful warrior is the average man, with laser-like focus.
> **Bruce Lee**

This not only gave a positive swing to the feedback, but put it in the future tense, implying that there would be a next time. Instead of making the person feel bad by saying, "You looked at your notes too much," which is in the past and points to what you felt they did wrong, we looked to the future with the expectation that they were doing well and that next time would be better, as well as giving them some ideas about how to accomplish it.

STRATEGIES FOR HAPPINESS

It is more powerful to be *for* something, than *against* it. Mother Theresa was once asked to join an anti-war rally. She responded, no, but if they were ever going to have a peace rally, she would be there.

I thought about this, and how it could be applied to my daily life. I want to think positively, I want to change my beliefs and I want to focus on what I want, not what I don't want. At the same time, I don't want to turn a blind eye to what bothers me because it bothers me for a reason and needs to be addressed.

Through using the evaluation technique, I have learned to evaluate my experiences with honesty. I can state what I really like about an experience or event, and when I get to what I don't like, state it in a manner that is forward-looking. Instead of saying, "I don't like the way I handled such and such," I will say "Next time, I'm going to be more sensitive and thoughtful, as I . . . ."

> The good life, as I conceive it, is a happy life. I do not mean that if you are good you will be happy; I mean that if you are happy you will be good.
>
> **Bertrand Russell**

If you have a hard time thinking of an alternative course of action, express it as you would like it to be. Michael Losier, author of *The Law of Attraction* (www.lawofattractionbook.com), says that in order to create positive vibrations, you should make statements such as this, "I love knowing that my ideal ___ is . . . ", or "I'm excited at the thought of . . ." or "I love how it feels when I . . ." Saying these statements allows you to be honest and at the same time, to focus on what you want to bring into your life.

Focus on What You Want

How about playing make believe? Create a *Vision Book*. Mike Dooley, author of the book *Notes from the Universe* (www.tut.com) suggests you create a book and fill it with pictures of places and things you want in your life. Write letters of "thank you" to yourself, paste positive quotes or anything that helps to create a mindset of what it would feel like to have had already accomplished your goals.

For instance, if you want to take part in a play, write a letter to yourself from the manager of the play, thanking you for all your hard work, and how your participation made the play such a success or write a positive review of the play, expounding on how it will be a smash success on Broadway.

Fill it with all sorts of imagery of how you want your life to be, and then look at it every day for at least 10 minutes and daydream. Make sure it stirs and excites you with joy when you look at it. Keep it fresh, often replacing items that no longer ignite your joy with something new. Not only will this keep your outlook and mindset positive and happy, but it will help you to move closer to achieving your goals. Include pictures that just make you smile, or even laugh out loud. The more positive the emotion it creates, the better your result.

These techniques may seem too simple to really be effective, but often it is those simple concepts that are the most powerful. So next time you are tempted to be negative, take a look at the thought. Your statement will reflect something in you or your life that you don't like or don't want. Stop and rephrase it to say what you would prefer to happen. Concentrate on thinking of ways you can make it happen. State in the future the *next time* scenario and, watch how your life changes.

Your Story

Amanda, my step-daughter, gave me a lucky bamboo plant for my 50th birthday. It consisted of seven stalks shooting up from a tray filled with pebbles. I was thrilled with the gift and so pleased and grateful that she took the time to think of something that would give me so much pleasure.

However, I am not the best person to take care of plants, and, as time went by, it began to wither. One by one, the stalks died. So much for my luck.

Except I don't believe in luck. I believe that we have the choice to create what is our life, for the good or bad. I created my own luck when I bought some new bamboo stalks and stuck them in the pot. So far, they are doing fine.

So, what are you going to do with your life? Are you going to surrender to what is – just accept that your life is dead and withered – or are you going to take action and develop your happiness potential? Are you going to just accept your present state of happiness, or are you going to take steps to improve your life? It's totally up to you.

As I stated at the beginning of this book, I am not out to fix you. Only you have the power and the right to take whatever actions you

YOUR STORY

need to make your life the fullest and richest it will ever be. There will be circumstances and events that are beyond your control, but you have full control as to how you are going to respond. You can choose to wallow in self-pity or jump in and enjoy the ride. This book is just one of many tools available to help you on your journey toward joy. For more reading ideas, take a look at the *Must Read Books* section on page 213.

I have shared with you strategies that can help you on your journey. They are just basic common-sense ideas. However, I know from experience that sometimes someone can say something in a chance conversation, or through an article or a book, and a light will come on. I often have one of those wonderful ah-hah moments that change the direction of my life. It is often so slight, I may not be totally conscious of it, but in the long run the effect is dramatic.

Allow yourself the opportunity to experience and express authentic happiness. If you still think it's selfish, then do it for your children. They will be better off with a parent who is positive, self-assured, radically humble, and . . . happy. Just think of the role model you can be to them. Your parents and spouse will appreciate that you are loving them because you can truly love yourself. Your friends will enjoy being with you because you are not a whiner and always feeling sorry for yourself. Most important, do it for yourself – because authentic happiness feels ***so good***.

I hope I have given you some ah-hah moments. I also hope you will lay down your burdens of fear, self-hatred, and self-pity to embrace the joy of being totally free. What will your story be? After all, when it comes to your story, you are the author. Get writing!

Hugs,   Donna

Desiderata

Go placidly amid the noise and the haste, and remember what peace there may be in silence.

As far as possible, without surrender, be on good terms with all persons.

Speak your truth quietly and clearly; and listen to others, even to the dull and the ignorant; they too have their story.

Avoid loud and aggressive persons; they are vexatious to the spirit.

If you compare yourself with others, you may become vain or bitter, for always there will be greater and lesser persons than yourself.

Enjoy your achievements as well as your plans. Keep interested in your own career, however humble; it is a real possession in the changing fortunes of time.

Exercise caution in your business affairs, for the world is full of trickery. But let this not blind you to what virtue there is; many persons strive for high ideals, and everywhere life is full of heroism.

Be yourself. Especially do not feign affection. Neither be cynical about love, for in the face of all aridity and disenchantment, it is as perennial as the grass.

Take kindly the counsel of the years, gracefully surrendering the things of youth. Nurture strength of spirit to shield you in sudden misfortune. But do not distress yourself with dark imaginings. Many fears are born of fatigue and loneliness.

Beyond a wholesome discipline, be gentle with yourself. You are a child of the universe no less than the trees and the stars; you have a right to be here. And whether or not it is clear to you, no doubt the universe is unfolding as it should.

Therefore be at peace with God, whatever you conceive Him to be. And whatever your labors and aspirations, in the noisy confusion of life, keep peace in your soul.

With all its sham, drudgery, and broken dreams, it is still a beautiful world. Be cheerful.

Strive to be happy.

by Max Ehrmann

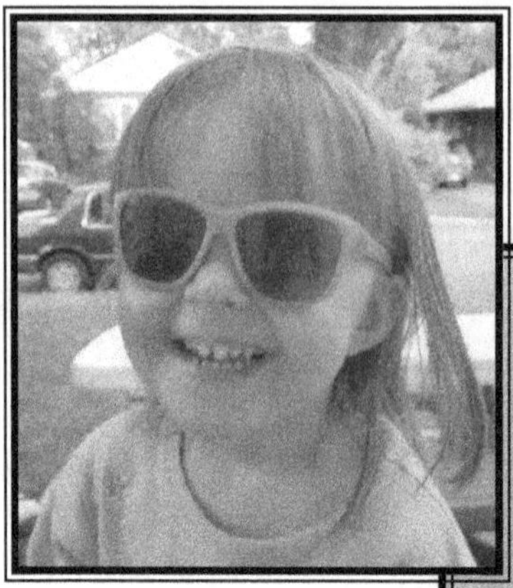
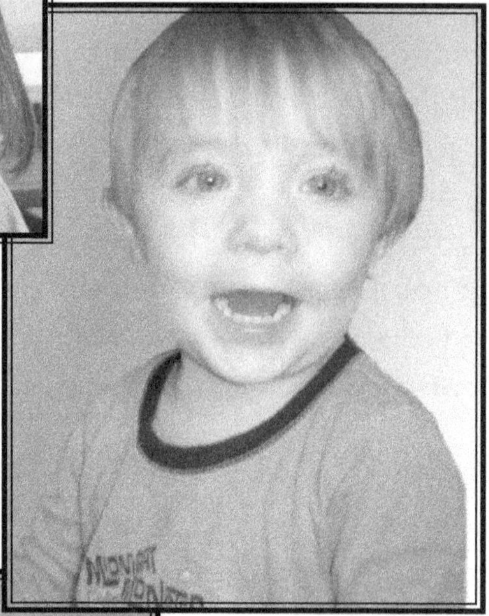
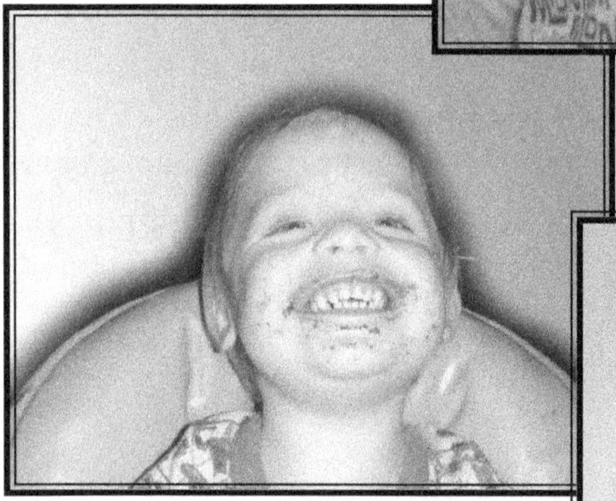
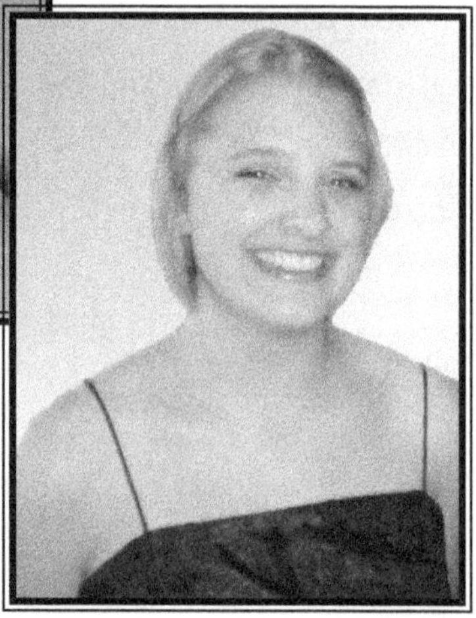

Must Read Books

The following is a list of many of the books I have read while doing research for this book. I highly recommend them to you.

Albom, M. (2003). *Five people you meet in heaven.* New York: Hyperion.

Albom, M. (1997). *Tuesdays with Morrie: An old man, a young man, and life's greatest lesson.* New York: Doubleday.

Baker, D., Stauth, C. (2003). *What happy people know: How the new science of happiness can change your life for the better.* New York: St. Martin's Press.

Baker, D., Greenberg, C., Yalof, I. (2007). *What happy women know: How new findings in positive psychology can change women's lives for the better.* New York: St. Martin's Press.

Burns, D., (1992). *Feeling good: The new mood therapy.* New York: Avon Books.

Chilton, D. (2002). *The wealthy barber: The common sense guide to successful financial planning.* Toronto: Stoddart.

STRATEGIES FOR HAPPINESS

Cudney, M.R., Hardy R. E. (1993). *Self-defeating behaviors: Free yourself from the habits, compulsions, feelings, and attitudes that hold you back.* New York: HarperOne.

Dalai Lama, Cutler, H.C. (1998). *The art of happiness: A handbook for living.* New York: Riverhead Books.

Dalai Lama, Cutler, H.C. (2005). *The art of happiness at work.* London: Hodder Mobius.

Dodd, R. (2006). *The power of belief.* Charlottesville: Hampton Roads Publishing Company.

Dooley, M. (2007). *Notes from the universe: New perspectives from an old friend.* New York: Atria Books/Beyond Words.

Dominguez, J., Robin, V. (1993). *Your money or your life: Transforming your relationship with money and achieving financial independence.* New York: Penguin.

Dyer, W.W. (1978). *Pulling your own strings.* New York: T.Y. Crowell Co.

Dyer, W.W. (2001). *Your erroneous zones.* New York: Avon Books.

Dylan, J. (2009). *The good life.* Mississauga: John Wiley & Sons Canada.

Eker, T.H. (2005). *Secrets of the millionaire mind: Mastering the inner game of wealth.* New York: Collins.

Ellis, A., Lange, A. (1996). *How to keep people from pushing your buttons.* New York: Carol Group.

Suggested Reading

Ellis, A., Harper, R.A. (1975). *A guide to rational living.* Boston: Wilshire Book Company.

Foster, R., Hicks, G. (2004). *How we choose to be happy: The 9 choices of extremely happy people–their secrets, their stories.* New York: Perigee Trade.

Frankl, V.E. (1997). *Man's search for meaning.* New York: Pocket.

Gilbert, D.T. (2006). *Stumbling on happiness.* New York: A.A. Knopf.

Glickman, R. (2002). *Optimal thinking how to be your best self.* New York: J. Wiley.

Hunt, M. (2008). *How To debt-proof your marriage.* Grand Rapids: Revel.

Hunt, M. (2003). *The complete cheapskate: How to get out of debt, stay out, and break free from money worries.* New York: St. Martin's Press.

Kaufman, B.N. (1994). *Happiness is a choice.* New York: Ballantine Books.

Keith, K.M. (2001). *Paradoxical commandments finding personal meaning in a crazy world.* Makawao, Maui, HI: Inner Ocean Publishing.

Losier, M.J. (2007). *Law of attraction: The science of attracting more of what you want and less of what you don't.* New York: Wellness Central.

McGraw, P. (2001). *Self matters creating your life from the inside out.* New York: Free Press.

Strategies for Happiness

Mundis, J. (2003). *How to get out of debt, stay out of debt and live prosperously*. New York: Bantam.

Nahirny, D. (2001). *Stop working . . . start living: How I retired at 36 without winning the lottery*. New York: Ecw Press.

Prager, D. (1999). *Happiness is a serious problem: A human nature repair manual*. New York: Harper Paperbacks.

Ruiz, M. (©1997). *The four agreements: A practical guide to personal freedom*. San Rafael, Calif: Amber-Allen Pub., Distributed by Hay House, Inc.

Seligman, M. (2002). *Authentic happiness Using the new positive psychology to realize your potential for lasting fulfillment*. New York: Free Press.

Seligman, M.E. (2006). *Learned optimism: How to change your mind and your life*. New York: Vintage.

Seuss, Dr. (1990). *Oh, the places you'll go*! New York: Random House Books for Young Readers.

Stevens, T.G. (1998). *You can choose to be happy: "Rise above" anxiety, anger and depression*. Seal Beach, CA: Wheeler-Sutton Publishing Company.

About the Author

Donna Hedley is a Speaker and Life Motivator based in Ottawa, Ontario, Canada. Holding a BRE in Education and Music from Emmanuel Bible College in Kitchener, ON, she is also a graduate of the Visual Developer Program at Willis College in Ottawa. In addition to that, she has obtained the Toastmasters CTM designation.

She co-wrote the book, *Ground Beef Creativity*, as well as articles about personal development, motivation, inspiration, and happiness. She has also developed and taught numerous courses in the Information Technology field.

Founder of the website ***www.Strategies4Happiness.com***, a web-site dedicated to helping others find their own personal happiness potential, she shares ideas and articles to inform and inspire. She also started ***www.SassySunflowerBooks.com*** to give authors the power to publish their own way.

As a motivational speaker, her message is positive, informative, and practical. As an IT Trainer, she is able to translate technical information into non-technical terms to communicate quality understanding for her clients. She is available for speeches, seminars and IT training. For more information visit ***www.DonnaHedley.com***.

Websites

43 Things

43Things is the world's most popular online goal setting community. Discover and list your goals. What do you want to do with your life? Track your progress by writing entries. Ask questions and talk with people who share similar goals.

www.43things.com

Authentic Happiness

Positive Psychology is a study of positive emotion, character traits, and institutions.

www.authentichappiness.com

Gratefulness.org

This international nonprofit organization provides resources for living in the gentle power of gratefulness, which restores courage, reconciles relationships, and heals our Earth.

www.gratefulness.org

Hoffman Institute

Provides extraordinary experiences for transformational change though the release of negative conditioning , accessing untapped resources of power, wisdom and creativity to discover your best self and make wanted changes in your life.

www.hoffmaninstitute.org

Institute of HeartMath

An internationally recognized nonprofit research and education organization dedicated to heart-based living – people relying on the intelligence of their hearts in concert with their minds to conduct their lives at home, school, work and play.

www.heartmath.org

Inspirational Words of Wisdom

An inspirational collection of words of wisdom in the form of poems, quotes, sayings, quote of the day, stories, thoughts, and motivation.

www.wow4u.com

Landmark Education

Provides training that is innovative and relevant that produces a fundamental shift in what is possible, to achieve higher standards of excellence personal lives, relationships, and wider communities of interest.

www.landmarkeducation.com

Law of Attraction

The science of attracting more of what you want and less of what you don't want.

www.lawofattractionbook.com

Learning to Forgive

Learn the steps to help overcome hurt feelings and grievances. Find out how you can improve your physical health and increase confidence.

www.learningtoforgive.com

Peak Potentials

Peak Potentials Training is a success and wealth training company.

www.peakpotentials.com

Thoughts Unique Thoughts

Use the power of thought and creative visualization to manifest dreams, create change and start over.

www.tut.com

You Can Choose to Be Happy.

100's of pages of on-line self-help personal growth information including complete copiesof Dr. Steven's publications.

http://www.csulb.edu/~tstevens/index.html

Give the gift of
Strategies for Happiness
How to Achieve Your Happiness Potential
to your friends and colleagues
Check Your Local Bookstore or Order Here

☐ YES, I want _____ copies of Strategies for Happiness: How to Achieve Your Happiness Potential.

☐ YES, I am interested in having Donna Hedley speak or give a seminar to my company, association, school, or organization. Please send me information.

Canadian orders: Include $21.00 cover price plus $7.45 shipping and handling for one book, and $2.25 for each additional book. Residents from Newfoundland and Labrador, Nova Scotia, New Brunswick and Ontario must add 13% HST. All other province must add 5% GST. Payment must be in CDN funds.

US orders: Include $17.00 cover price plus $5.45 shipping and handling for one book, and $1.95 for each additional book. Colorado, Ohio and New York residents must include applicable sales tax. Payment must be in US funds.

International Orders: Include $17.00 US cover price plus $10.00 US shipping and handling for one book, and $3.95 US for each additional book.

Payment must accompany orders. Allow 3 weeks for delivery.

My cheque or money order for $ _____ is enclosed.

Name _____

Organization _____

Address _____

City/State/Zip _____

Phone _____ E-mail _____

Signature _____

Call (613) 799-1017
Make your cheque payable and return to:
Sassy Sunflower Books
PO Box 67106
421 Richmond Road
Ottawa, ON K2A 4E4

www.S4HTheBook.com/order.php
www.SassySunflowerBooks

CPSIA information can be obtained
at www.ICGtesting.com
Printed in the USA
LVHW111137240320
650967LV00001B/1